GERMAN JEWS
BEYOND JUDAISM

THE MODERN JEWISH EXPERIENCE

Paula Hyman and Deborah Dash Moore, *editors*

Lavater and Lessing Visit Moses Mendelssohn, a paint-
ing by Moritz Oppenheim, signed and dated 1856.
Mendelssohn is playing chess with Johann Caspar La-
vater. Standing is the writer and dramatist Gotthold
Ephraim Lessing. Courtesy of the Judah L. Magnes
Memorial Museum, Berkeley, California.

George L. Mosse

GERMAN JEWS
BEYOND JUDAISM

Indiana University Press • BLOOMINGTON

Hebrew Union College Press • CINCINNATI

This book is based on the
Gustave A. and Mamie W. Efroymson Memorial Lectures
delivered at the Hebrew Union College-Jewish
Institute of Religion in Cincinnati, Ohio,
in April 1983.

First Midland Book edition 1985.
Copyright © 1985 by Hebrew Union College Press

Library of Congress Cataloging in Publication Data

Mosse, George L. (George Lachmann), 1918–
    German Jews beyond Judaism.

    (The Modern Jewish experience)
    Based on the author's Efroymson lectures at Hebrew
Union College.
    Bibliography: p.
    Includes index.
    1. Jews—Germany—Intellectual life.   2. Germany—
Intellectual life.   3. Germany—Ethnic relations.
I. Title.   II. Series: Modern Jewish experience
(Bloomington, Ind.)
DS135.G33M59 1985   305.8'924'043   84-42841
ISBN 0-253-32575-7 cl.
ISBN 0-253-20355-4 pa.
1 2 3 4 5 89 88 87 86 85

CONTENTS

PREFACE   ix

I. A Cultural Emancipation   1
II. German Jews and German Popular Culture   21
III. Intellectual Authority and Scholarship   42
IV. A Left-Wing Identity   55
V. The End and a New Beginning?   72

NOTES   83
INDEX   95

PREFACE

What started as the Efroymson lectures at Hebrew Union College has become a book. When I was invited to give these lectures, they seemed an excellent opportunity to analyze a heritage which has both fascinated and puzzled me over a long period of time. Students at the University of Wisconsin in the 1960s first brought the present-day attraction of this heritage to my attention; courses in European cultural history were filled with young people searching for a new identity. For many, the ideas discussed in this book came as revelation—supplying an inspiration which their own American tradition had somehow failed to provide. I have had similar experiences in Germany in recent years. Some of the German ideas which had provided German-Jewish intellectuals with their identity were familiar, but their Jewish context was all but forgotten.

This book is meant as an introduction to a German-Jewish identity destined to remain relevant. It points to German culture in the age of Jewish emancipation as first providing a German-Jewish identity; it was subsequently an inspiration for many men and women searching to humanize their society and their lives. It also shows how intellectual and articulate Jews drifted out of the mainstream of German culture and politics into an intellectual isolation even before the Nazi seizure of power. Such isolation might have remained without consequence except for the use made of it by the German political right. This book can also be read as a study of the German *Bildungsbürgertum,* implying more than the English "cultured bourgeoisie"—the social group to which so many German Jews belonged and within which they played a controversial role.

I want to express my specific gratitude to the late Uriel Tal for many discussions on this topic over the years. David Sorkin's description of *Bildung* has largely determined my own analysis of this important concept. The holdings on the history of German Jewry of the National and Hebrew University Library in Jerusalem have proved inexhaustible, and it has been necessary and pleasant to consult the libraries of the Leo Baeck Institute in New York and Jerusalem as well. Without the friendship and encouragement of Paul Breines, this book would not have been written at all.

GERMAN JEWS
BEYOND JUDAISM

I

A Cultural Emancipation

To DISCUSS once more the German-Jewish dialogue seems superflous at best, an effort to recapture a history which seems to have failed. While some claim that the dialogue never took place at all, and others believe that Jews had a large space in which to become Germans, both seem to have missed the most important fact about this dialogue, which, in a truly unprecedented fashion, became an integral part of the European intellectual tradition, in spite of its apparent failure after the Nazi seizure of power. For example, the German-Jewish dialogue largely determined what we perceive as Weimar culture (although this was only one of its aspects)—Jews interacting with Germans on many levels of art and literature. Twenty years after the collapse of the Third Reich, students throughout the western world returned to that tradition in their search for a better society, an alternative to the constraints imposed upon the individual. Although this dialogue did not affect all German Jews in equal manner—those in the city more than those in the country, the articulate minority more than the inarticulate majority—most were touched by its ideal of self-cultivation and liberal outlook on society and politics, based upon the need to transcend the gulf between their own history and the German tradition—to stress what united rather than divided peoples and nations. The German-Jewish dialogue with which we are con-

1

cerned not only served to produce a unique heritage for the Jews themselves and for intellectuals all over Europe, but also became a part of the German-Jewish identity, infiltrating to some extent most aspects of Jewish life in Germany.

The Jews were a small minority in Germany, never much more than 1 percent of the total population, and while Germany between 1871 and 1933 grew from 41 million to about 65 million, the Jewish population hovered between 500,000 and 600,000.[1] It was this tiny minority which entered into a dialogue with the majority. The very term "dialogue" connotes a conversation between equals, and the German-Jewish dialogue was such a conversation at times. I prefer, however, to define "dialogue" as an interaction on different intellectual levels, not necessarily equal (which seems to me irrelevant and difficult to define in this context) but always without giving up one's own identity—Germans as Germans and Jews as German Jews. That Jewish identity had to be redefined, as Jewish emancipation led to Jewish assimilation, did not mean a rejection of that identity, as is often asserted in retrospect; German Jews were for the most part fully aware of their Jewish origins. As a 1930 article in the journal of the Central Association of German Jews *(C. V. Zeitung)* put it, we must place the highest value on humanity as a whole, while at the same time loving the German people and our specific Jewishness.[2]

What, then, was the nature of this dialogue and the reason for its great attraction for German Jewry and for others, later, who lived long after its end? The answer to that question, as I will attempt to present it, transcends the specifically Jewish and German; it lies in the search for a personal identity beyond religion and nationality. I will first ask why important and articulate German Jews in interaction with their German environment embarked upon the search for such an identity—and when they thought it established, clung to it until the bitter end. Then I shall ring some important variations upon this theme—how German Jews attempted to connect with the German people, to German popular culture; the new kind of scholarship which grew out of this search; and, finally, the characteristics of the peculiar left-wing identity that emerged, although liberalism continued to be the political home of most Jews.

The timing of German-Jewish emancipation determined the

definition of Jewishness. Jews were emancipated during the first decade of the nineteenth century in the autumn of the German Enlightenment. This gave them their optimism, a certain faith in themselves and in humanity. *Sulamith,* the journal founded in order to speed up the process of Jewish emancipation, wrote in 1811 that the "people of Abraham, fighting against obstacles of all kinds are working their way upwards to humanity."[3] From darkness to light—that theme of liberalism and, later, of socialism—was deeply ingrained in German Jewry. But if the Enlightenment made Jewish emancipation possible, gave it a faith and an aim, it also supported an ideal of self-education which was decisive for the history of German Jewry.

Jews were emancipated at a time in German history when what we might call "high culture" was becoming an integral part of both German citizenship and the Enlightenment. The word *Bildung* combines the meaning carried by the English word "education" with notions of character formation and moral education.[4] Man must grow like a plant, as Herder put it, toward the unfolding of his personality until he becomes an harmonious, autonomous individual exemplifying both the continuing quest for knowledge and the moral imperative.[5] Goethe's *Wilhelm Meister's Apprenticeship* (1795–96) summed up this ideal in one phrase—"the cultivation of my individual self just as I am" (*"mich selbst, ganz wie ich da bin, auszubilden"*).[6] Such self-education was an inward process of development through which the inherent abilities of the individual were developed and realized.[7]

The term "inward process" as applied to the acquisition of *Bildung* did not refer to instinctual drives or emotional preferences but to the cultivation of reason and aesthetic taste; its purpose was to lead the individual from superstition to enlightenment. *Bildung* and the Enlightenment joined hands during the period of Jewish emancipation; they were meant to complement each other. Moreover, such self-cultivation was a continuous process which was never supposed to end during one's life. Thus those who followed this ideal saw themselves as part of a process rather than as finished products of education. Surely here was an ideal ready-made for Jewish assimilation, because it transcended all differences of nationality and religion through the unfolding of the individual personality.

Herder had already envisioned the concept of *Bildung* as a means of overcoming the inequality between men. He wanted to level the differences between the bourgeoisie and the aristocracy by confronting the nobility with an ideal which would deflate its pretensions.[8] The instrument used to abolish the inequality between bourgeois and aristocrat might also work to transcend the differences between the German and the Jewish middle classes. The centrality of the ideal of *Bildung* in German-Jewish consciousness must be understood from the very beginning—it was basic to Jewish engagement with liberalism and socialism, fundamental to the search for a new Jewish identity after emancipation. The concept of *Bildung* became for many Jews synonymous with their Jewishness, especially after the end of the nineteenth century, when most Germans themselves had distorted the original concept beyond recognition.

Berthold Auerbach, considered by his fellow Jews to be one of the most representative German Jews of the nineteenth century, wrote that "formerly the religious spirit proceeded from revelation, the present starts with *Bildung.*"[9] His *Schrift und Volk* (*The People and the Book*, 1846) called for religion to become *Bildung*— "an inner liberation and deliverance of man, his true rebirth; not through words or customs, but through his deeds, his character, the totality of his life, the cleansing and healing of all human labor."[10] Generations later, from exile in London in 1939, Rabbi Ignaz Maybaum lamented that while during the Weimar Republic someone who did not believe in the prevalent concepts of God could still be considered a man of culture, today, he wrote, such a man can choose only "barbarism or faith."[11] Judaism had become a position of last resort in a world increasingly deprived of *Bildung*.

That German Jews so wholeheartedly accepted the ideal of *Bildung* as a new faith suited to their German citizenship was a result of their social structure. German Jewry contained a small upper class which corresponded to the various levels of the gentile middle class, but most Jews were poor (Jewish beggars were not unknown), and others lacked a steady source of income. Perhaps because they were without roots in any established class or occupation, it was relatively easy for most of them to embrace the ideals and goals of the bourgeoisie into which they had been emancipated.[12] However, unlike the German middle class, Jews had no organic or family ties to the lower classes and no experience with German popular piety and German popular culture.

For example, Berthold Auerbach, as the author of the popular *Black Forest Peasant Tales (Schwarzwälder Dorfgeschichten, 1843)*, enjoyed an unprecedented esteem and popularity among Jews and gentiles alike. Auerbach was born in a village, but when he came to define the nature of peasant society in his *Schrift und Volk*, his peasants reflected a middle-class outlook on the world. Those who live on the land, he tells us, regard life not as a means to find pleasure but as directed by a sense of duty, where righteousness prevails and action is based on reflection.[13] Auerbach's peasants are assimilated into bourgeois society as they break out of their nar-row regional vision and religious bigotry. After all, whatever one's class or station in life, "the development of the human spirit knows no boundaries and cannot be confined by religious dogma."[14] To be sure, Jews seldom appear in his village stories, and never as ped-dlers, which was the way many villagers encountered Jews. The few Jews in his stories were usually teachers or merchants at the periphery of village life and yet existing harmoniously side by side with the peasants.[15] At one time, when anti-Semitism was on the rise, Auerbach wanted to write a story about a Jewish village (after all, such villages existed in Germany) but gave up without explana-tion,[16] perhaps because such a subject was not congenial to one committed to transcending religious differences through *Bildung*.

Small wonder then, that Auerbach's popularity declined hand in hand with the original ideal of *Bildung* and the Enlightenment— his *Dorfgeschichten* were eventually forgotten. The taste of the bourgeoisie changed, and as the twentieth century began, they wanted to read about peasants who exemplified the ideal of rootedness in the nation which they had made their own. Now it was Hermann Löns's *Der Wehrwolf* (1910) which pre-empted the popularity once granted to Auerbach's village stories. Here the peasants symbolize the elemental forces of Germanic nature, coursing beneath the surface, as they defend their land during the Thirty Years War; cruelty was accepted as a part of everyday life.[17] Löns exalted a German peasant type quite different from the peas-ant boy in Auerbach's *Barfüssle (The Girl without Shoes, 1856)*, who repudiated all thoughts of revenge against his persecutors and left his village harboring ill will toward no one. *Bildung* and the

Enlightenment, the substance of Auerbach's Jewishness, respected during the nineteenth century, were being repudiated at the beginning of the twentieth.

Several presuppositions of the Enlightenment were basic to the concept of *Bildung*—the optimism about the potential of human nature and the autonomy of man; the belief that acquired knowledge would activate the moral imperative; and, last but not least, the belief that all who were willing to use and develop their reason could attain this ideal. "The possession of a higher *Bildung* is the knighthood of modernity,"[18] and, unlike the medieval knighthood, one which Jews as well as gentiles could attain. As *Sulamith* wrote, "If we talk about equality, then its meaning must focus upon man's potential, if we deny the equal potential of man, then all equality vanishes."[19] It was the degree of a person's *Bildung,* not his religious or national heritage, which ultimately decided the degree of equality.

The quest for harmony was basic to the concept of *Bildung* in a Germany touched by the industrialization of Europe, frightened by the French Revolution. The aesthetic was the keystone of that harmony, linking the intellectual and the moral. That this should have been the case is difficult to understand in our own time, when beauty has become relative and the aesthetic is either regarded as a luxury or trivialized into the knickknacks of daily life. But during the late eighteenth and the nineteenth centuries, writers such as Wilhelm von Humboldt, who elaborated the concept of *Bildung,* stood under the powerful influence of the Greeks. Ancient beauty seemed to give form and direction to individual and communal ideals. The classics provided the modes of thought and taste essential to the cultivation of the personality. The aesthetic was linked to the intellectual faculty, and both activated the moral imperative which resided in every man.

The beautiful as the essence of aesthetic education was not romanticized but understood through reason, as lean as Greek sculpure itself. The beautiful, in accordance with the Greek ideal, was conceived as harmonious and well proportioned, without any excess or false note which might disrupt its quiet greatness. Beauty was supposed to aid in controlling the passions, not in unleashing them, emphasizing that self-control which the bourgeois prized so highly. The ideal of Greek beauty transcended the daily, the momentary; for Humboldt, as for Goethe and Schiller, it symbolized the ideal of a shared humanity toward which *Bildung* must strive. This beauty was a moral beauty through its strictness and harmony of form; for Schiller it was supposed to keep humanity from going astray in cruelty, slackness, and perversity.[20] *Bildung* was not chaotic or experimental but disciplined and self-controlled.

Artists and writers could play a key role in pointing the way to true *Bildung*. For example, Goethe understood his role in society as that of an educator, and so did Schiller in his *Über die ästhetische Erziehung des Menschen (The Aesthetic Education of Mankind*, 1795). Indeed, some of the most important German-Jewish writers continued this tradition; precisely because they were writers, they had a special mission to educate their fellow citizens in *Bildung*. Eventually, they became the custodians of the classical concept of *Bildung* when toward the end of the nineteenth century many Germans attempted to nationalize and romanticize it—to see beauty as a substitute religion that consoled, reconciled, and saved—beauty as truth, as holy.[21] To later Germans, beauty satisfied emotional needs rather than strengthening rationality and self-discipline.

The classical concept of *Bildung* largely determined the post-emancipatory Jewish identity. "He who wants to be filled with a sense of beauty," Humboldt tells us, "must have clarity of consciousness."[22] The concept of *Bildung* was on one level an attempt to keep control in the midst of social and political disruption, but on another level, through its emphasis on aesthetics, it reflected the fact that the nineteenth century was becoming an increasingly visually oriented age as the largely illiterate masses were integrated into politics and culture through the use of symbols—from cheap reproductions of pictures to national monuments. The Jews were eventually the losers here, as it proved easy to attack their emancipation through the creation of visual stereotypes. But at first they benefited from this development, for the concept of *Bildung* seemed ready-made for their needs—everyone could attain *Bildung* through self-development and education. Goethe, for example, held that men were born with an innate drive toward *Bildung*. *Bildung* made it easy for Jews to "embrace Europe," as *Sulamith* put it.[23] Thus, in Hamburg in 1837, Rabbi Gotthold Salomon praised King David as a man of *Bildung* and concluded that without self-control no human greatness or virtue was possible. Even more typical, perhaps, Ludwig Philippson's journal for rabbis and Jewish schools made a sharp distinction in 1834 between the ceremonial culture of the ancient Jews and modern *Bildung*.[24]

The Jews, unlike the masses, reached for *Bildung* in order to integrate themselves into German society. The Jews and the German masses entered German social and political life at roughly the same time, but the Jews were apt to reject the world of myth and symbol, the world of feeling rather than reason. Through the very process of their emancipation, they were alienated from the German masses. The struggle for *Bildung* itself played an important part in this alienation. Humanity, wrote Humboldt in 1792, has attained a level of culture from which it can progress only forward through the self-cultivation of individuals. Thus all institutions which hinder this self-cultivation, which transform men into the masses, are harmful. Humboldt used this argument to warn against the interference of the state in the process of education. Humboldt's educational ideal, which, as Prussian minister of education (1809–10), he wanted to put into practice in the gymnasium as well as at the newly founded University of Berlin, joined students and professors in an academic community based solely upon mutual self-cultivation through learning.[25] Yet in spite of the religious tolerance which was supposed to prevail among those engaged in the process of *Bildung*, the contrast between the individual and the masses, the cultured bourgeoisie and the many so-called uncultured men and women, was a potential menace to Jewish assimilation. They were in danger of isolation through their consistent commitment to Humboldt's *Bildung* rather than to that nationalized and romanticized concept of self-cultivation which had managed to pervade popular piety and culture.

Jews were emancipated not only into the bourgeois world of *Bildung* and the Enlightenment but also into the German wars of liberation against Napoleon. Jews were patriots attempting to document their emancipation and new citizenship by enlisting in these wars, and Moritz Oppenheim in 1835 painted a Jewish volunteer returning home from the war in order to celebrate the sabbath with his family. For the first time in Germany, Jews were portrayed by a Jewish artist, and in a manner which linked Jewish religious observance to German patriotism. But in the picture the patriotic overshadows the Jewish ritual, and both are embedded in a scene of middle-class family life.[26]

The Jewish community of Berlin exhorted its departing soldiers, "Never forget that all warriors are part of a common humanity."[27] German nationalism itself was still at the crossroads in these wars, and until the occupation of Prussia by Napoleon, patriotism and cosmopolitanism were often joined, and even fanatics of German unity like the poet Klopstock held that Germans were ennobled by their tolerance toward other peoples.[28] When the anniversary of the Prussian victory over the French at the battle of Leipzig was celebrated all over Germany in 1814, there was a feeling of pride that Jews joined in the singing of Christian chorales during the celebrations and that "cultured" men and women rejoiced in the victory of German arms without regard to their religious differences.[29] Patriotism retained its eighteenth-century meaning of solidarity rather than domination.[30]

Ernst Moritz Arndt, whose numerous writings exhorted Germans to fight for their freedom against the French, equated German freedom with the freedom of all mankind.[31] Yet at the same time he wrote with contempt about those Germans whose patriotism was similar to the religion of Nathan in Lessing's *Nathan der Weise (Nathan the Wise,* 1779)—one which loved the whole world while those at home were left to freeze in the cold.[32] This attack on the Magna Charta of German Jewry served a purpose—the Jew as a cosmopolitan *Bildungsbürger* was made into a symbol for a commitment to *Bildung* and the Enlightenment that was said to have caused Germany's defeat by the French—and previously enlightened thinkers such as Fichte, under the growing weight of nationalism, came to share this outlook. However, German Jews by and large did not follow the example of patriots turned nationalist. After all, men were transformed into citizens by the enlightened concept of *Bildung,* not by an emotional appeal to nationalist myths and symbols.

Once man had begun his self-cultivation, Humboldt believed, he would spontaneously enter political life as the culmination of this process. Individual freedom was of the essence, and Humboldt used the example of Greece, where citizenship and individuality had been identical[33]—the Greeks were "too noble, sensitive, free and human" to tolerate any interference with the unfolding of the human personality.[34] Here, then, was another aspect of *Bildung* bound to appeal to the newly emancipated—citizenship was not contrary to individual freedom; indeed, citizenship could not exist without individual freedom. "The further modern *Bildung* progresses," wrote Berthold Auerbach, "the more it is based upon the individual who from out of his own unique personality joins the state."[35] What counted was individual self-cultivation and the network of personal relationships.

The process of emancipation and with it the growth of autonomy of the individual became a reality for many Jews through personal friendships. The eighteenth-century cult of friendship in Germany was part of the ideal of *Bildung* itself—differences of personality and character must be recognized and then submerged in a common effort at self-cultivation. For example, Goethe's *Wilhelm Meister's Apprenticeship*, whose definition of *Bildung* was cited earlier, saw man's greatest happiness in friendships consisting of giving and receiving out of each friend's richness of personality developed through mutual self-cultivation.[36] Lessing, in his drama *Die Juden* (*The Jews*, 1749), has a Jew say to a stranger whom he has met on his travels, "I saw that although you indicated hostility toward my nation [the Jews], you were favorably disposed toward me. And a man's friendship, whoever he be, will always be invaluable to me."[37]

Such an ideal made a substantial contribution to Jewish emancipation; indeed, many contemporaries saw this process as part of the cult of friendship. Moses Mendelssohn was usually pictured walking or talking with his Jewish and Christian friends. Moritz Oppenheim painted him in the company of Lessing and Lavater (see Frontispiece). The poet Wieland greeted Mendelssohn "in the sacred name of friendship,"[38] and so did others who wanted to accept the Jew as an equal. Berthold Auerbach, reflecting the Jewish attitudes of his time, wrote in 1839 that it was through friendships with men such as Moses Mendelssohn that humans are distinguished from animals.[39] The ideal of friendship went deep, and we shall come across the tendency to personalize all relationships once more when we consider how some German-Jewish writers attempted to carry the concept of *Bildung* to the German people.

When Ludwig Geiger, toward the end of the nineteenth century, reflected on the literary salons which had existed in Berlin almost a century earlier, where Jews and Christians had freely associated with each other, he saw such friendships not as a temporary bond but as a solid and durable chain linking Christians and Jews.[40] Jews were apt to idealize such friendships; for example, in 1812, Joseph Wolf saw personal friendships as the paradigm of the relationship between God and man.[41] No single factor seemed to symbolize the threat from the new wave of anti-Semitism of the 1880s better than the sacrifice of personal friendships to so-called higher considerations of religion, race, or nation, as some Christians broke off their friendship with Jews.[42] No other single factor can better characterize both the liberalism and the socialism of German Jews than their desperate efforts to preserve or to restore the autonomy of personal relationships.

The fate of *Bildung*, friendship, and Jewish emancipation was determined by historical forces whose importance seems clear in retrospect, even if contemporaries were unaware of their significance. The concept of *Bildung* was created by a new class reaching for power. For the bourgeoisie, it fulfilled two vital functions—it helped legitimize the middle class compared to the upper and lower classes, and it facilitated the creation of a bourgeois elite which, as Humboldt intended, would provide better civil servants for the Prussian state. Jews were emancipated into a bourgeoisie which needed the concept of *Bildung* for its own ends. This did not mean that it was taken lightly; it became an article of faith, a striving toward greater things as an integral part of bourgeois existence. With the passage of time, *Bildung* itself, like its aesthetic component, became detached from the individual and his struggle for self-cultivation and was transformed into a kind of religion— the worship of the true, the good, and the beautiful.[43] Thus Theodor Fontane, the gentle critic of bourgeois society, wrote about his Jenny Treibel in 1892: "She's a dangerous person and all the more dangerous for not really knowing it herself, and she sincerely imagines that she has a feeling heart . . . for 'the higher things.' But she has a heart only for what has weight . . . that counts and bears interest."[44]

Bildung as a means of gilding bourgeois materialism—this was not the ideal Jews had so readily embraced. However, the original ideal of *Bildung* had never sufficed to establish the restraint and control which were of the essence for bourgeois society. From the very beginning, nationalism had come to the rescue in order to reinforce the cohesion of society against the onslaught of modernity. A certain vagueness had always plagued the concept of *Bildung*. At the beginning of the nineteenth century, Fichte had put forward a definition of *Bildung* which reappeared much later in Friedrich Paulsen's classic *Das Deutsche Bildungswesen* (*German Culture*, 1912)—*Bildung* was a means of reshaping reality through the power of ideas—but, Fichte added, ideas rooted in the German character.[45] Jews clung to the idealism of *Bildung* and seem scarcely to have realized that both bourgeois society and the people themselves needed more tangible signposts in order to make the abstract concrete. The history of German Jews from one point of view is that of chasing a noble illusion, but in that process, many political and scholarly perceptions were reshaped. How typical it was that a German Jew, Ernst Bloch, in exile from National Socialism, wrote that without daydreams and the building of castles in the air the world would never be changed.[46]

Daydreams and castles in the air could cope with neither the pressures of Germany's abrupt industrialization nor the always latent danger of the revolt of the masses. *Bildung* had to be adjusted to the imperative of keeping control over public and private life. Discipline and conformity, in the last resort, took precedence over self-cultivation and spontaneity of citizenship. Indeed, the so-called *Volksschule*, in which the great majority of Germans received a rudimentary education, always required submission and docility. But then Humboldt was interested only in the elite gymnasium and the university.[47] *Bildung* should have been open to all those willing and able, but soon the ideal was controlled by a self-perpetuating elite. *Bildung* was institutionalized in the gymnasium and the university, to be controlled by the mandarins—the full professors at the university and, at a great distance, the professors at the secondary schools. The university as the "conscience of the nation" maintained academic freedom, perhaps better in Wilhelminian Germany than in the years before German unification. This freedom produced astounding results—more through research than teaching—and propelled Germany to the forefront in the sciences and humanities. Yet most professors, as *Praeceptor Germaniae*, claiming to be the conscience of nation, in reality became the guardians of the existing order. Even if some professors led movements for social and political reform and helped to prevent the introduction of censorship in Wilhelminian Germany, the alliance between professors and bureaucrats restricted any open-endedness—it was the product and not the process of education which counted.[48] Patriotism, duty, and discipline threatened to replace the critical mind of the Enlightenment, a prerequisite for the self-cultivation of man. What remained of *Bildung* was characterized by Ludwig Marcuse, who, writing about his teachers at the beginning of the twentieth century, said that they "worshipped Prussian army barracks adorned with Doric columns and Corinthian capitols."[49]

This change was gradual but accelerated in the last decades of the nineteenth century. In 1804, Friedrich Schleiermacher, perhaps the most influential Prussian clergyman, under the influence of pietism and the wars of liberation, had warned the so-called cultured Germans not to regard the state as merely a negative factor in German life (as, in fact, Humboldt viewed it) but instead as a moral authority. The fatherland gives the highest meaning to life. At the same time, Fichte began to see in the state the sole moral, political, and economic force which must shape and control the mass of individuals that comprise it.[50] Jews had been excluded from academic life and from the civil service at the very beginning of their emancipation in spite of the promise of equal rights. Humboldt had made no distinction between Jews and Christians as he described the new bourgeois elite. But a century later, in 1909–10, less than 3 percent of the full professors at German universities were Jews—that is, had penetrated the mandarins.[51] As the concept of *Bildung* changed and compromised with the new nationalism, as conformity was demanded instead of continuous individual self-cultivation, the Jews were increasingly isolated.

That individualism which had provided an anchor for Jews reaching out to Germany was in danger of being cut loose. What had happened to the ideal of friendship, so crucial for Jewish assimilation, was typical of a new, sterner age. Nationalism claimed dominance over personal relationships. Fichte's assertion, made during the French occupation of Prussia, was to gain general acceptance toward the end of the nineteenth century—man could not love himself or anything outside himself unless ideas rooted in the

German character were part of the system of belief.[52] Once such systems of belief were regarded as more important than the free choice of friends and personal self-cultivation, romantic, pietist, and patriotic traditions combined to exclude as "outsiders" those who had not shared the German historical experience. As the nineteenth century progressed, fewer German *Bildungsbürgers* used the popular word *"Geist"* in order to describe the critical mind engaged in making empirical discovery through the use of reason; instead, they saw the mind as identical with the *volk*—the soul. The Greeks were thought by some to provide immutable beauty only inasmuch as they gave form and content to the German national stereotype.[53] Together with the transformation of *Bildung* into a new kind of religion, these factors helped erode the common ground between the German and German-Jewish *Bildungsbürgers* which had once seemed so certain and promising.

This erosion of the classical concept of *Bildung* was not sudden but gradual and never complete; it gained its full momentum only after World War I. Yet the new anti-Semitism of the 1880s was not only a Jew-hatred stimulated by an economic depression, the maladjustments of industrialization, and the menace from unruly classes and impatient youth; it had deeper and longer-lasting roots. On the surface, this was the Indian summer of the bourgeois world and Jews had never lived more comfortably in Germany. In reality, their isolation was being prepared and their role as "outsider" established.

Although many Jews accepted the changed demands of society, however uneasily, many others clung stubbornly to the older ideal of *Bildung*. The quarrels and divisions among Jews were, with the exception of a very few Zionists and a minority of the orthodox, fought upon a shared commitment to the ideal of *Bildung*. Sometimes it seemed that regardless of their religious or political conviction they might have joined the young Walter Benjamin in praise of his friend Ludwig Strauss's statement that "above all, in a study of Goethe one finds one's Jewish substance."[54] Translated into the way of life of the Jewish *Bildungsbürgertum*, this meant that "quotations from Goethe were part of every meal."[55] Kurt Blumenfeld, the Zionist leader, argued in 1914 that a Jew who understood German culture and had made Goethe, Fichte, and Keller a part of his life would more easily acquire Jewish national consciousness.[56] This statement, in turn, is not far removed from Ernst Bloch's belief that true Marxism was the heir of that humanism which informed the bourgeois during its classical period—the age of Goethe and Humboldt.[57] The optimism so much a part of the earlier ideal of *Bildung* was alive among Jews who had, after all, seen many of their hopes fulfilled. As the liberal Rabbi Caesar Seligmann wrote, "From a martyr the Jew has become a bourgeois."[58]

Reason and culture were perceived as bulwarks against reaction, and Jews found allies in many educated Germans. There were those, Jews and Germans, who until the very day of the Nazi seizure of power were convinced that someone as uncultured as Hitler could never attain high office in Germany—culture had that special meaning for Jews which was shared by some, but no longer most, middle-class Germans.

Lessing's play *Nathan the Wise* was and remained the Magna Charta of German Jewry, the popularization of *Bildung* and the Enlightenment. The play was thought to provide a clear statement of Lessing's love for humanity regardless of religion, a love exemplified by his close friendship with Moses Mendelssohn. Hannah Arendt calls Lessing the classical writer on friendship. For Lessing, friendship meant conversation keeping humanity alive in dark times.[59] Gabriel Riesser, one of the first Jews to enter German politics and in 1848–49 vice-president of the Frankfurt parliament, wrote that with Lessing we attain a new phase of *Bildung*, a "heavenly bliss." He went on that during Lessing's lifetime, humanity awakened from its slumber in order to strive toward "justice and compassion, beauty and *Bildung.*"[60]

During the 1880s, Jews led the subscribers to Lessing monuments as a confession of faith, according to the *Allgemeine Zeitung des Judentums.*[61] Much earlier, Gabriel Riesser, in his call to erect a Lessing monument, had counseled contemporary Jews to look to a more recent rather than to their faraway past. They should ask themselves in any given situation what Lessing would have done.[62] So much for the relevance of the Bible or a specific Jewish tradition, and that from a religious Jew, a leader of the Hamburg temple! What, after all, was Jewish about Nathan? Was it that he was a rich merchant or that his family was killed in a pogrom? To most Jews, it was his *Bildung*—his wisdom and tolerance—which counted. This could be interpreted as allowing for diverse religions provided they dedicated themselves to serve all of humanity. At Lessing's two hundredth birthday in 1929, the official newspaper of the largest German-Jewish organization (the *C.V. Zeitung*) praised Lessing both for his ideal of a perfect and united humanity and for his refusal to dissolve religious differences into merely an ethical culture. Lessing, so we read, teaches how one can be a believing Christian or Jew and yet fuse one's faith with the religion of humanity, "just as one can be simultaneously a German and a citizen of the world."[63]

At the same anniversary, the theater critic Julius Bab warned German Jews not to exaggerate Nathan's importance—after all, he never existed and was a mere phantom of the poetic imagination.[64] Yet, in 1933, when, excluded from German cultural life, the Jews founded their *Jüdische Kulturbund* (Jewish Cultural Organization), it was Julius Bab, as director, who decided to inaugurate its first season with a performance of *Nathan the Wise* in order to encourage that "great German culture which gave us nourishment."[65] Even so, the Nazis on this occasion forced the *Kulturbund* to issue an explicit denial that it sought to keep alive the true German spirit among the Jews. This performance was a confession of faith, more meaningful than the subscription to the Lessing monument. Nathan's Jewish identity was given a new emphasis through the production, although it was hoped without in any way diminishing the play's basic message of tolerance and universalism. Thus Nathan is made to hum a Hasidic tune in the first act, and a menorah and a prayer stool graced with a Star of David were placed in his house. Still, it was the change of emphasis at the end of the play which caused the most comment—even Lessing has Muslim and Christian leave the stage arm in arm, newly adopted relatives, while Nathan makes a separate although happy exit. In the 1933 production, however, Nathan stayed behind, proud and lonely at the front of the stage, as the curtain fell.[66]

The Zionists on the whole were satisfied with a performance they had opposed as merely repeating assimilationist themes. But in this performance they saw their ideals closely tied to specific groups and peoples, apparently corresponding to their contention that the nation was a necessary stepping-stone toward humanity. Nevertheless, the *Kulturbund* had far to go if it wanted to repudiate the assimilationist past. However, the *Central-Verein deutscher Staatsbürger jüdischen Glaubens,* by far the largest organization of German Jews, took the opposite stand—Nathan's loneliness belied his joyful belief in God and negated the lessons of the play, which joins different peoples together through their common humanity and mutual tolerance.[67] Here the optimism, the faith in the potential of man, was still intact, though the German-Jewish dialogue no longer existed and the Jews had become the sole custodians of Humboldt's ideal of *Bildung.*

The defeat in the First World War and the difficult transition from war to peace heightened the tendencies toward the irrational in German life. The start of the Weimar Republic was as turbulent and noisy as its end fourteen years later was miserable but quiet. The concept of *Bildung* became an ever narrower vision in the hands of the German political right: nationalist and racist, yet proud of its educational and cultural status. The Aryan race alone was said to possess the depth of feeling which *Bildung* required; only Aryans could understand the meaning of the good, the true, and the beautiful.

Many, perhaps most, Germans, did not yet agree with such pretensions; the classical ideal of *Bildung* was not so quickly defeated. Perhaps there was still hope, even after the war, and in this situation some Germans, and above all some of the most prominent German Jews active in political life, attempted to redress the growing irrationality of German public life by turning to France for support. The nation which had been the home of the Enlightenment, and which had rehabilitated Captain Dreyfus within recent memory, might yet redress the balance in Weimar Germany. For example, Theodor Wolff, the famed editor of the *Berliner Tageblatt,* wanted to model the newly founded Democratic Party on the French Radical Socialists; his ideal state was the Third French Republic. Georg Bernhard, the editor of the rival *Vossische Zeitung,* had a similar vision.[68] Modris Ekstein's study of the major democratic newspaper in Germany, owned and largely written by Jews or men of Jewish descent, concluded that these were journalists in the tradition of the French *philosophes.*[69] No sooner had the war ended than Hans Lachmann-Mosse, the proprietor of the *Berliner Tageblatt,* in a purposeful gesture of reconciliation, brought Yvette Gilbert to Berlin in order to sing French *chansons* in the

German capital. This preoccupation with France demonstrates the lack of realism on the part of those who hoped that the defeat would be easily forgotten, that the lessons learned from the war would lead to a restoration of reason and enlightenment. These German Jews were joined by men such as the novelist Heinrich Mann, who in 1918 believed that the intelligentsia on the one hand and the people on the other would proceed to build a "republic of reason."[70]

Such lack of realism in politics was strikingly characteristic of the Jewish bourgeoisie. It must be explained in large part by their commitment to a German-Jewish identity which no longer corresponded to the realities of German life. Not only were German Jews faced with an increasingly narrow vision of *Bildung*, but the primacy of culture had been one of its unintended consequences. Theory came first, and politics was subordinated to culture. For example, *Sulamith* in 1806 explicitly exalted *Bildung* above all pragmatism.[71] The Jewish leadership during the Wilhelminian Empire believed for a long time that liberal politicians would, as a matter of course, put principles before politics. Thus they ignored the frequent overt and tacit alliances between liberals and anti-Semites.[72] And so it would remain, for Jewish liberals as well as for those Jewish socialists for whom criticism of culture was of much greater importance than analysis of the political economy.

Yet because the concept of *Bildung* was built upon theory rather than practice, it easily provided a new identity for many articulate and intellectual German Jews, for despite its emphasis on the individual and the critical mind, it could be lifted into immutability and become a secular religion. After all, the eighteenth-century Enlightenment had elevated nature into an immutable if rational force which directed men's search for truth. Humanity was seen as an abstraction, a moral imperative, which made all men equal—endowed with identical virtues and rational minds. The religion of humanity had indeed become a secular faith, not dependent upon revealed religion—a faith, however, which took nothing on trust and whose truths were discovered only by a critical mind constantly refined through self-cultivation.

The new self-identity of the German Jews was expressed within a framework that gave it form and discipline and served to transcend Judaism and Christianity. For example, speaking before the *Central-Verein* in 1910, Rabbi Cossmann Werner of Munich castigated Jews who had been baptized into Christianity for committing a crime not merely against Judaism but above all against humanity itself. Such Jews opposed equal rights and hindered others in fighting for justice, for "to be a Jew means to be human," a statement which was greeted with thunderous applause.[73] The argument against baptism was based not on Judaism as a revealed religion but on the religion of humanity. The sermon itself was reprinted during World War I as part of the so-called front-line library published by the Central Association of German Jews.

German Jews, especially those committed to *Bildung,* attempted to reach out to the German people; in their desire to educate them, they followed a general trend among intellectuals excluded from the world of mandarins. Such a trend was, after all, also a part of the original concept of *Bildung,* where everyone— not just a closed and self-perpetuating elite—was thought capable of reaching the goal. Some Jewish socialists wanted to join the German working class, but once they had done so, they were often singled out as troublesome intellectuals who refused to do their duty as foot soldiers in the workers' movement. Others, scholars for the most part, ignored the masses and attempted to exorcise the irrational by examining it rationally and dissecting it in the rational mind. They were to initiate new ways of analyzing history and philosophy. The Jews who seemed to have the greatest success in reaching out were those writers who, before World War I and during the Weimar Republic, sought to transmit the classical ideal of *Bildung* through their best-selling novels or biographies.

Stefan Zweig became perhaps the most famous of these writers. Although he was Austrian by birth, he must be discussed as a German writer, for his works became part of the popular culture of Germany. Zweig was proud that he knew no nations, only individuals—that his interest focused on humanity as a whole.[74] He attempted to infuse his works with a liberal spirit, one based on *Bildung,* but which at the same time made the abstract concrete so that it might be widely understood. Making the abstract concrete meant viewing all issues from a private rather than a public perspective. Such an approach to contemporary problems was not apolitical, as some have recently charged,[75] but part of Zweig's belief in the primacy of individual development and personal relationships as a prerequisite for the very existence of German Jewry. Nor was his belief in humanity as naive as it appears to some modern commentators; instead, he continued the tradition of the Enlightenment.[76] Zweig was not alone; the historian Emil Ludwig, now forgotten, was equally popular. Others also tried to reach out, always trying to make popular literature relevant in order to change the perceptions of the German people—to put up a dike against the wave of nationalism and confrontation politics engulfing Germany.

The preceding discussion of *Bildung* has given us the nineteenth-century foundation for understanding the dilemmas and frustrations of twentieth-century German Jewry. It is from the mountain of a classical *Bildung* that these intellectuals descended to the people before and after World War I, hoping to find them ready for the message. If their success was largely illusory in immediate terms, in the long run they presented an attractive definition of Jewishness beyond religion and nationalism.

II

German Jews and
German Popular Culture

GERMAN JEWS were emancipated into a Germany of *Bildung* and the Enlightenment whose ideals were being transformed by the narrowing horizons of German life. Yet under the Wilhelminian Empire, the isolation of German Jews was latent rather than real, and the overwhelming majority of Jews lived comfortably as members of German bourgeois society. With the founding of the Weimar Republic after World War I, all discrimination against Jews ended and their full emancipation was finally achieved. Jews were prominent in Weimar culture and, at first, entered Weimar politics as well. But what seemed the realization of full and equal citizenship, the dream of previous generations, in reality proved to be a decisive stage in the increasing isolation of the Jews in Germany.

A decade after the founding of the Weimar Republic, political parties of all colors avoided, if possible, nominating Jews for public office, and the "Jewish question" had become an integral part of the political discourse, assuming threatening dimensions which it had not possessed earlier. The Jews were the victims of the confrontational politics, the near civil war, of the last years of the Weimar Republic—they became the foils of mass movements of the right and even the left in politics. Moreover, republican Germany was the main battleground in Europe between the modern movement and the forces of tradition in literature, the theater, visual arts, and certain currents in music. The polarization of politics was accompanied by a polarization of culture. Jews seemed to take sides—indeed, to play a visible and crucial role in encouraging the modern rather than the traditional.

What today we are apt to call Weimar culture was largely the creation of left-wing intellectuals, among whom there was such a disproportionate number of Jews that Weimar culture has been called, somewhat snidely, an internal Jewish dialogue. These intellectuals were themselves looking for roots, often reaching out to the German people, whom they were apt to define as the working class. Their dilemma will occupy us later, but the high visibility of Jewish socialists fueled the quite unjustified belief that Jews were anti-national and had turned their backs on the defeated and humiliated German people. However, some of the most important Jewish intellectuals who wanted to make contact with the German masses did not believe that the working class was the appropriate medium. They wanted to reach out to the German people through popular culture, to clothe their message in forms which required no historical or philosophical learning. It is with their attempt to make contact with the German people, to help shape their culture, that we will be concerned in this chapter.

The polarization of German politics and culture locked many Jews into liberal and socialist positions, for anti-Semitism had closed the door to the political right. Jews did join parties such as the Catholic Center Party and the *Volkspartei* which had succeeded the National Liberals—parties which had a conservative bent but which supported the republic. However, Jews who wanted to join with those who called themselves conservatives during the Weimar Republic, in the *Deutschnationale Volkspartei* or in smaller conservative political circles, were less fortunate, despite a plea for admission by one Jewish conservative, who pointed out that successful conservative parties like the English Tory Party and the Italian Fascists knew no anti-Semitism. Instead, the inquiries of Jews who wanted to vote in 1932 for the *Deutschnationale Volkspartei,* at that time closed to them, were either ignored or answered positively only after the election was over.[1] Political reality reinforced the inclination of German Jews to support liberal causes. Jews did welcome the new in culture; as a group, they were much more open to experimentation than the German *Bil-*

dungsbürgertum. Thus Jews sent their children to experimental boarding schools such as Wickersdorf, founded by the radical school reformer Gustav Wynecken (where in 1922, 40 percent of the student body were Jews),[2] and supported avant-garde culture as both patrons and audience. Indeed, at the end of the nineteenth century, Aubrey Beardsley in England had satirized the fascination which the newest in art and literature held for rich German Jews through an opulent and corpulent Jewish audience in his black-and-white sketch of "Male and Female Wagnerians at a Performance of Tristan and Isolde." Some Jews had indeed supported the Wagner "festivals" at Bayreuth,[3] although there a love for the new in music may have been less important than proving one's German identity by adopting the Wagnerian myth. However, during the Weimar Republic, such support was no longer given to a political and cultural right which condemned all experimentation and which, unlike Richard Wagner, consistently matched its anti-Jewish rhetoric with the exclusion of Jews from its midst.

The tradition of *Bildung* was important here as well. Even those who personally had little in common with the avant-garde or left-wing intellectuals remained relatively interested in the new and the experimental as necessary to the process of intellectual growth. For example, the editors of the prominent liberal press, the men who ran the *Berliner Tageblatt,* the *Vossische,* and the *Frankfurter Zeitung,* while themselves of more catholic tastes, opened their pages to the newest in music, literature, and the arts. This reaching out to the new was reflected even in a classic analysis of the meaning of Judaism itself. Leo Baeck's *Das Wesen des Judentum (The Essence of Judaism,* 1906) invoked the example of Jewish messianism against what he called the *Kulturzufriedenheit*—satisfaction with the cultural status quo—and called Judaism the yeast among the people, a ferment of decomposition.[4] No bridge could lead from such a dynamic concept of Judaism to the growing German political right. Support for the avant-garde, for the new in culture, for what is called Weimar culture, in short, was built into the German-Jewish tradition of *Bildung* and the Enlightenment. Over a century had passed since emancipation, but the need to be accepted as equals, to find common ground between German and Jew, had not changed, nor could it change. This meant a constant effort to transcend German historical traditions which Jews could not claim as their own. Some, such as Auerbach, cut the German peasant loose from his local and provincial roots in order to give him a wider vision; most others supported cultural innovations, where the past would no longer haunt an enlightened present.

Moreover, those German Jews engaged in intellectual pursuits, the producers of culture, were until 1918 largely excluded from the world of mandarins and thus were pushed into what were regarded as marginal professions—journalism, the arts, the theater, and free-lance writing.[5] They continued to crowd these professions under the Weimar Republic. Whether consumers, patrons, or creators of avant-garde culture, Jews were continually being cast in the role of outsiders through their engagement with modernity. To be sure, they found many like-minded Germans to share their quest, and here, on the margins of established and conventional society, a true German-Jewish dialogue took place. Jews, however, already isolated from the German masses, were committed to the pursuit of a higher culture, making contact with the masses increasingly difficult. Yet it was precisely their involuntary role as outsiders which left a heritage much more meaningful to future generations than that left by the insiders. Nationalist and right-wing literature tends to be provincial, and in Germany it was the logical descendant of nineteenth-century writers, who, obsessed with their Germanic roots, had isolated German literature at a time when French and English writers were read all over the world.

Left-wing intellectuals, avant-garde artists, liberal journalists, and free-lance writers were puzzled, hurt, and angered by the lack of popular support, by the failure of the German people to respond to their efforts. They regarded their task as educational, but the victory belonged instead to those who were able to mobilize the masses—not only by promising their liberation but by appealing to more traditional patterns of thought.

Some Jewish writers did become popular in a manner closed to left-wing intellectuals, avant-garde artists, or the liberal press. Their books reached millions. However, it is unlikely that their work penetrated much beyond the middle class, although most of their books were serialized, cheaply priced, and found in popular lending libraries. Writers such as Stefan Zweig and Emil Ludwig meant not merely to entertain but to educate, to spread the ideals of *Bildung,* to encourage the exercise of a critical mind. These men were liberals in the old tradition; for example, like the liberal press, they rejected the militant patriotism of World War I. The substance of their Jewishness, as they saw it, was expressed through their cultural stance, just as it was for many other Jewish intellectuals and many Jewish patrons of German culture.

Men such as Zweig and Ludwig were progressive but not avant-garde, and that was part of their strength as popular writers. They were not far ahead of their times, and for all their commitment to *Bildung* and the Enlightenment, a certain nostalgia for continuity in life and politics informed their work. To be sure, Zweig believed that life should be lived passionately, but he regarded sustained passion as unhealthy—ending either in death or in a return to so-called normal behavior.[6] *Bildung* and the Enlightenment were permeated by overt or implied praise for the middle-class style of life. Here there was no avant-garde predilection for shocking the bourgeois or any left-wing attack upon their lifestyle. Emil Ludwig, for example, pleaded for a balance between pleasure and accomplishment which would keep eroticism in check.[7]

Such writers provide a good illustration of what happened when *Bildung* and the Enlightenment attempted to reach out to popular culture. And the history of German Jews raised a concurrent larger problem—how a high culture which was individualistic, humanist, and pacifist could interact with popular culture. Emil Ludwig and Stefan Zweig have been singled out in the discussion above, but they were not alone; others shared their approach. All of these writers stood in the tradition of German Jewry, and an analysis of their work points to a particular German-Jewish heritage, a Jewish substance beyond religion and nationalism. The favorite literary medium for both Zweig and Ludwig was historical biography, perhaps reflecting the search for the individual in a Germany whose politics seemed to shift with the sway of the irrational masses. Their writings during the Weimar Republic, their attempt to reach out to the people, to overcome Jewish isolation, must be placed within an already established German-Jewish tradition. Berthold Auerbach in his *Schrift und Volk* had idealized the German people; Zweig and Ludwig were to follow his footsteps over half a century later. Each individual, endowed with the potential for good rather than evil, carries the collectivity upon his shoulders, Auerbach tells us. The more that men and women subordinate the national and the regional to general human concerns, the more perfect the community in which they live[8]. Auerbach reflected the optimism of the Enlightenment and *Bildung*, and so did the popular Jewish writers during the Weimar Republic. Auerbach's attempt to form a unity out of diversity, to unite regional traditions with those of the nation and all of humanity, were continued by Stefan Zweig, who liked to join together the most unlikely characters in his collective biographies.

Between 1911 and 1938, Emil Ludwig's popular biographies sold 1.2 million copies in Germany, 1.1 million copies in the United States, and 800,000 copies in the rest of the world.[9] Ludwig's name became a household word in the most unexpected places. Thus, when I entered England as a young refugee student and the Dover customs official found out that I studied history, his immediate reaction was, "Another Emil Ludwig?" Indeed, for the Nazis, Emil Ludwig symbolized the so-called Jewish decomposition of German culture, another tribute to his popularity. His real name was Emil Ludwig Cohen, and his father had encouraged him to drop the Cohen in order to have a better chance at a professional career. Ludwig had neither a Jewish nor a Christian education; straightforward moral teaching had to suffice, as he wrote in his autobiography. Why, he asked, should one fill the mind of any European child with the history of desert tribes foreign to his very nature?[10] Ludwig took the logical step and converted to Christianity but for only a short time. Shocked at the murder of Walther Rathenau, he left the church in protest against the hatred for Jews which had led to the murder of one of Germany's finest men, saying, "I feel a new attachment to my race, now that it once again suffers persecution in the fatherland." Ludwig was indifferent to religious dogma; God, nature, and Goethe, he said, determined his faith.[11] His conversion to Christianity had been merely an effort to buy the respect of Germans. Whether in or out of the church, he saw himself as having a mission to educate his readers in rationality and tolerance—to proclaim that autonomy of the individual so crucial to the concept of *Bildung* and the Enlightenment.

Stefan Zweig, an equally popular writer, was a more concerned Jew than Emil Ludwig, although he also was brought up in a very lax fashion in matters of faith.[12] As a convinced although belated pacifist during World War I, he wrote to Martin Buber in 1916 that Jewishness must never lead to a retreat behind bars—a separation from the world—and that instead it represented an opportunity for world citizenship.[13] Somewhat later in the war, he asserted that all nationalism, all narrowness of vision, must be rejected; it was the mission of Judaism to demonstrate the existence of a spiritual community which did not depend on the quest for territory.[14] He remained faithful to these ideals after the war as well. They were, in fact, built upon a definition of Jewishness whose substance was *Bildung* and the Enlightenment; neither Zweig nor Ludwig felt the need for traditional religion. Their Jewishness was a search for a personal identity beyond nationalism and religion, and from this quest they sought to influence the German people.

Zweig, like Ludwig, wrote historical biographies, but wrote novels and short stories as well, although the biographies were of special relevance for his self-appointed educational task. Readers hungered for history after World War I, for personality and leadership. The urge to follow a leader in times of crisis, which was to have such fateful political consequences, also helped to popularize historical biographies. These centered on well-known men for the most part, statesmen such as Napoleon or Bismarck or writers such as Goethe or Byron, who had become cult figures. Ludwig's fame dated from his *Bismarck,* published before the war (1911) and described by his publishers on its cover as something new—not the work of a politician or a historian but of a psychologist who built upon history. The human personality was examined in isolation; historical forces which might have helped determine men's actions were ignored, and only man's inner life and his self-development counted. Zweig wrote that the masses could not grasp abstract thought; man himself must be substituted for the idea as a tangible symbol.[15] Both Ludwig and Zweig, unlike those usually associated with Weimar culture, had an insight into needs of popular culture, but neither wanted to use this insight to build national monuments.

Ludwig's biographies were critical up to a point; his biography of William II (1924) blamed the emperor for having started

World War I,[16] just as the arrogance of individual statesmen was given responsibility for the failure to keep the peace in July 1914. Ludwig wrote that if he could dissolve historical analysis into a personal dynamic, then the teacher, the barman, and the seamstress would be gripped by Bismarck's ambition and striving.[17] Historical research was not necessary for his "word pictures," Ludwig tells us; enough secondary sources existed based on scholarship. "The artist, not the scholar, is called upon to paint portraits as an example or as a warning for his age."[18] The historical method followed by Ludwig and Zweig was best described by a critic of another popular biography, written in England, where this genre proved equally popular after the war. Lytton Strachey's *Eminent Victorians* (1918) lowered a small bucket into the great sea of documents and came up with characteristic specimens—a world where the whole could be deduced from its parts.[19] But in this case the specimens were meant to disillusion rather than to educate and were informed by a cynical spirit rather than the urge to spread *Bildung* and Enlightenment. For Zweig and Ludwig, the driving forces of history were individual character and fate. History creates decisive moments, Zweig tells us—minutes in which the fate of men and nations are decided.

These biographies attained a mass readership because of the way they were constructed—history was transformed into a drama, narrated with breathless intensity. Stefan Zweig titled his most successful book *Sternstunden der Menschheit* (*Tides of Fortune*, 1927) and added additional biographies to it in each new edition. For example, the history of the entire nineteenth century was said to have been determined in the few minutes it took General Grouchy to make the decision that Zweig believed lost the Battle of Waterloo for Napoleon.[20]

The conclusions of these biographies were usually satisfactory, if not always happy. Thus, as portrayed by Ludwig, Lord George Byron and Ferdinand Lasalle, subjects of a double biography, led stormy lives, yet both died at just the right moment—at the height of their explosive energies. If they had lived, their subsequent lives would have been anticlimatic. Similarly, Walther Rathenau was murdered at the proper point of his life, when all signs pointed to his fall from power.[21] In these biographies, a robust optimism accompanies the drama of life—history works for the best, the good in human nature triumphs over the bad.

The only Jew thought worthy of a popular biography side by side with Napoleon or Bismarck was Walther Rathenau. It is interesting to consider the extent to which Rathenau became a powerful model for German Jews. He seemed a symbol of the Weimar Republic, for which he sacrificed his life—as the official journal of the Berlin Jewish community put it—of its potential for true equality between Germans and Jews.[22] For Ludwig and Zweig, he symbolized the unity through diversity which was their ideal, as it had been Berthold Auerbach's shortly after emancipation. Rathenau, Zweig tells us, combined knowledge, action, and a stupendous *Bildung*.[23] He succeeded, Ludwig writes, beyond the dream of any Jew, but even in success he was lonely, betrayed by all around him; his was a "strength out of weakness," reflecting the position of Jews in Germany.[24] Zweig was more direct—Rathenau symbolized the loneliness and grandeur of the Jewish spirit, which lacked the easy consolation of religious faith.[25] Both writers thought that Rathenau's death was the logical consummation of his life, for he could have gone no further. The portrait which emerges is built upon Rathenau's Jewishness defined through the power of intellect rather than faith. But, then, Rathenau himself had written that the cultivated Jew depends upon dogmatic religion less than any other contemporary man of culture.[26]

Rathenau not only exemplified Jewish contributions to Germany but also symbolized Jewishness expressed through an active life inspired by learning, self-cultivation, and friendship. Ludwig and Zweig were not alone in emphasizing that no matter how busy, Rathenau found time for conversation with young friends.[27] No mention is usually made of Rathenau's German nationalism or of his Jewish self-hatred. He became a role model for German Jews to a greater extent than most rabbis or community leaders, until the emergence of Leo Baeck as a leader under the Nazis. But even Leo Baeck, although a man of profound religiosity, was perceived and looked upon himself as a man of culture.[28]

The attempt to educate, to spread the concept of *Bildung*, was never far beneath the surface in the biographies of Zweig and Ludwig. German genius, Ludwig tells us, was never political but always cultural, and Bismarck was made to exemplify to the world that rationalism and open-mindedness characteristic of true culture.[29] Dogmatism was the enemy, as it had been for Berthold Auerbach so long ago, and it made little difference that Ludwig, unlike Auerbach, was several generations removed from the process of Jewish emancipation. Writing about Goethe and Schiller, heroic figures of German culture, Ludwig discussed the differences between them; nevertheless, they were united in their rejection of nationalism and ancestor worship. Patriotism, clericalism, and aristocracy, Ludwig tells us, had seen their day.[30] These words could have been written to good effect a hundred years earlier; by 1924, when they were published, the liberalism for which they stood was sadly outdated. It seems almost bizarre, in retrospect, that Stefan Zweig wrote a biography of Erasmus (1934) in order to protest the intolerance and confrontational politics of his time. Humanism, he wrote, was constantly threatened by passion.[31]

Both Zweig and Ludwig were doomed to disappointment. Zweig's increasing bitterness eventually ended in suicide, but Ludwig's reaction to the Third Reich was more complex and differentiated. His love for biography threatened to end in uncritical admiration for strong leadership. He had always believed in the existence of genius, a natural consequence of his concentration upon individual character. When he interviewed Mussolini and Stalin, a note of respect and awe crept into his description of the dictators. Their accomplishments were emphasized in order, so we are told, to paint a realistic picture. Yet his admiration for Mussolini and Stalin was a consequence not so much of misplaced realism as a journalist's temptation to swim with the tide, facilitated by his individualistic approach to history. "He for whom history is formed by personalities," Ludwig wrote in his *Führer Europas nach der Natur gezeichnet* (*Leaders of Europe,* 1934), "must find a government of four hundred mediocrities more alien than the rule of one outstanding dictator." But in the same breath he prophesied the end of nationalism and condemned the warlike education of youth.[32] Such inconsistency under the pressures of National Socialism demonstrated an unease with the ideal of *Bildung,* its earlier roots now irretrievably lost. It was not easy to stand alone in front of the stage when everyone else has left it. Ludwig's ambivalence about Mussolini and Stalin was a consequence of his failure to influence the German people through his own ideals, even though he had sold millions of books.

Zweig remained more consistent, summing up in 1937 what Jewishness meant to him: "I did not wish Judaism to repudiate its universalism and supranationalism in order to retreat into its Hebrew and nationalist past . . . I believe that the Jewish and the human substance must remain identical."[33] The Jewish reinforced the human; indeed, this was its primary task. Much earlier, Emil Ludwig, writing in Martin Buber's journal *Der Jude* (1925), had called his fellow Jews not the salt but the pepper of Europe in their idealism and commitment to European unity.[34] Both writers stood on essentially the same ground and conceived their task in similar ways. When Austria was annexed to the Nazi Reich, Stefan Zweig wrote, referring to his *Erasmus* of four years earlier, "We are too Erasmian . . . to prevail against these men who have a battering ram in place of forehead and brain. Against those possessed by the mania of nationalism only those themselves possessed can stand: we are poisoned by our humanity."[35]

The ideal of humanity was to be passed on to the German masses, and both Ludwig and Zweig did attract a new readership—men and women who had been without books. They captured a popular audience, made contact with the German people, but most read their books as one might read a good detective or adventure story. The mass sale of books frequently bore little relationship to their effect. Thus, Erich Maria Remarque's anti-war novel, *Im Westen nichts neuese* (*All Quiet on the Western Front*, 1929), was one of the runaway best sellers of the Weimar Republic. The German right launched a concerted onslaught against the book and against the film based on it but without much success. Yet they need not have worried, for the book had no discernible political impact. The playfulness and conspiratorial delight of Remarque's young soldiers meant that the book could be read as a schoolboy's adventure story.[36] Ludwig and Zweig were able to write according to popular taste, and here they were successful but only at the cost of their message.

Their failure to achieve their objective, and the reasons for this failure, illustrate the further isolation of German Jews in Germany. The attitude of Ludwig and Zweig toward the masses is significant, for it derived from the ideals which the cultivated middle class had embraced during the age of Jewish emancipation but was fast relinquishing in favor of the community of the *Volk*. Emil Ludwig, in his life of Christ, *Der Menschensohn* (*The Son of Man*, 1929), one of his least successful books, pits Christ the moralist against the masses eager to see him crucified. The masses, Ludwig tells us, always cry for blood and will do so two hundred years from now.[37] Concentration on individual character necessarily consigned the masses to a subordinate role; they became little more than extras in the unfolding drama.[38] Ludwig, like most *Bildungsbürger* of his time, feared the leveling power of the masses. He condemned both the alliance between Social Democrats and the Army, which crushed the radical revolution in 1919, and the revolution itself. Instead, he declared, the spirit unarmed must revolutionize the wage slaves and unite all nations. The true enemy was the newly awakened militarism.[39] Here Ludwig was close to some left-wing intellectuals and their ideal of a revolution brought about by the activation of the categorical imperative within men and women, without violence or the use of force.

Stefan Zweig looked with horror at what he considered the demonic masses. For him, the popular enthusiasm which accompanied the early stages of World War I was reason betrayed to passion. The revolution which followed was an expression of the impure drive for power by corrupt individuals. He feared that because so many Jews were revolutionary, a wave of anti-Semitism would follow.[40] Ludwig and Zweig, like Berthold Auerbach before them, attempted to diffuse the masses by dissolving them into their components. Personal friendships were the only human bonds which Zweig recognized. Humanity, he believed, will progress toward universality not as a mass but as individuals.[41]

This paring down of the masses was a concept in direct conflict with the main political and cultural currents of the postwar years. The longing for leadership which helped popularize Ludwig's and Zweig's biographies was itself part of the search for a meaningful faith around which Germans could unite, into which they could retreat, during those crisis years. The mobilization of the masses through national myths and symbols and the ideal of a leadership which shared a belief in such myths and symbols were foreign to Ludwig's and Zweig's way of thinking. Moreover, the primacy of culture, inherent in the concept of *Bildung*, served to alienate them still further from popular culture and popular politics. Stefan Zweig sensed this growing isolation when he wrote to Emil Ludwig in 1925, "Sometimes I am oppressed by the feeling

that we who possess an encyclopedic knowledge, men who passionately work at extending their *Bildung,* are already a kind of
fossil."[42]

Just as Ludwig and Zweig reduced the masses to their individual components, so did they also distinguish between culture
and politics—as potential outsiders, they seem to have feared any
totality as homogenization. Thus, Stefan Zweig's biography of
Joseph Fouché (1929) was, as he wrote, "a book against politics
which have no faith in ideas, in other words the politics of Europe
today."[43] Zweig felt that culture must determine politics and that a
high moral purpose must inform political life.

The commitment to culture as the guardian of morality excluded overt political action; individual *Bildung* would in the last
resort solve all problems of life. Ludwig never entered politics, and
Zweig prided himself on being a so-called unpolitical man.[44] Zweig
never voted and refused to sign protests against National Socialism
for fear that they would be considered political acts. The only way
to react to the crisis, he wrote in May 1933, was through silent and
tenacious perseverance.[45] Zweig had been a militant pacifist during
World War I, and both he and Ludwig supported the Weimar
Republic. But their weapon was culture, not politics. Such a distinction ran counter to the popular wish for fully furnished houses
and the felt need for a civil religion which would integrate all
aspects of life.

Ludwig and Zweig symbolized the alienation of the German-
Jewish tradition from popular culture. They could not see past
their own ideals to fathom the wishes and desires of the people.
Their conviction that the moral, spiritual, and intellectual
capacities of individuals determined events was deeply held and
thus not easily shaken. Yet, for all that, tolerance, compassion, and
broadness of outlook were not unknown to German popular culture. Indeed, writers of immense popularity in the late nineteenth
and early twentieth centuries, such as Marlitt (Eugenie John) and
Ludwig Ganghofer, had attacked religious dogmatism, exalted the
dignity of the individual, and advocated toleration of the Jews.
Popular literature in Germany was largely liberal, as exemplified
by *Die Gartenlaube,* a journal which at its height had the unparal-
leled circulation of half a million copies and which, for most of its

history, was devoted to perpetuating the tradition of the revolution of 1848. *Volk*ish and anti-Semitic literature never attained equivalent popularity.[46]

Reading *Die Gartenlaube*'s praise for Lessing's *Nathan the Wise* and its eulogy for Kant because he exalted reason,[47] one might think that Ludwig and Zweig should have encountered fewer obstacles in their efforts to influence popular culture. But the ideals of German popular literature did not stand in isolation; they were joined to popular culture's quest for a faith which would encompass all of life and would provide shelter and security. The liberal current of German popular culture was linked to its apparent opposite through a revolutionary tradition which had become deeply rooted in Germany. The apocalyptic view of history gave hope that a new dawn was about to break, that the scourges which preceded the rule of God would be overcome, and that eternal justice would prevail. Paracelsus and Jacob Böhme were the principal prophets of the "underground revolution," to use Ernst Bloch's term, or the "German revolution," as it was called by the German political right in order to distinguish it from the French Revolution.[48]

This apocalyptic tradition had inspired William Weitling and his Communist League (which Karl Marx found in place when he started his life's work), just as Ernst Bloch attempted to harness it to the left in *Thomas Müntzer* (1921). But this revolutionary tradition strengthened the right rather than the left, for the divine unity between God and nature, central to the apocalyptic vision, was best exemplified by the German *Volk* as an ever-present utopia. A Germanic continuity was said to exist which would break through, make time stand still, and abolish death. At that point, a new dawn would unleash the potential in each individual and create a society of decency and tolerance. But before that could happen, the enemy had to be slain—the country had to pass through times of trouble before the thousand-year Reich could begin.[49]

The liberal utopia of popular culture was postponed until the end of time. Meanwhile, the way would be prepared by eliminating the Jews and other outsiders from German life and waging war against Germany's enemies. Hitler was needed so that the fairy tale could begin. "The work which took a thousand years to accomplish, which the greatest Germans merely saw through the eyes of the spirit, [was] about to be accomplished" through the self-

sacrifice of the few and the deeds of one, Adolf Hitler.[50] Thus the
Third Reich did not yet exist but was always about to become real
and dominate the earth, as had been prophesied in the Book of
Daniel. The usefulness of the German revolution to explain un-
popular political action and to mobilize the masses was obvious,
and it further strengthened a political right which could make full
use of this tradition.

The ideals of Stefan Zweig and Emil Ludwig bore no relationship to this revolutionary tradition, and there is no evidence that
they recognized its force. The ideal of *Bildung* and the Enlightenment, the moral imperative which accompanied them, was antago-
nistic to this deep stream of popular piety. Yet some German Jews,
such as Ernst Bloch and Martin Buber, understood its portent and
sought to harness it in their own thought. Bloch himself, for all his
later popularity, was isolated among left-wing intellectuals. Starting with his *Thomas Müntzer* (1921), he attempted to use the
apocalyptic tradition to give Marxism an explosive vision, radical
hope, and openness toward the "not-yet."[51] These visions of hope
were to inspire, not replace, the class struggle. In contrast, Martin
Buber attempted to fuse this Germanism with a Jewish tradition. It
was no accident that Buber wrote his doctorate on Jacob Böhme,
demonstrating the continuing relevance of German mysticism.
Whatever the connection with the Jewish tradition of Buber's
work on the Hasidim, which began to appear in 1906, it was partly
inspired by this "underground revolution." The Hasidic stories
stimulated great enthusiasm among young Jews just before World
War I, precisely because here they had found a Jewish popular
culture which could quell their hunger for myth. Buber provided a
congenial Jewish tradition already familiar through the German
mystics. He tidied up the distasteful ghetto past by equating Jewish
mysticism with a respectable German mystical and apocalyptic
tradition, laundering the Hasidim for their use by the emancipated. The young Georg Lukács suddenly discovered that he
might be of Hasidic descent, and under their influence, Walther
Rathenau became, for a short time, an avid student of Hebrew.
These were highly assimilated Jews who had no intention of turning their backs on Germany.[52] The argument could be made that by
assimilating a Jewish to a German tradition, Buber's Hasidim had
the best of both worlds, although on one level the German domi-

nated the Jewish because of the literary style in which the stories
were written.

These Hasidic stories represented an alternative to the major
trends of the German-Jewish tradition, as exemplified by Stefan
Zweig and Emil Ludwig. Buber himself was aware of this. The
traditional concept of *Bildung,* he wrote, was solely future-
oriented, but a point of departure was as important as a point of
arrival.[53] This perceptive criticism seemed warranted during the
Third Reich when Buber addressed the problem, yet it was precisely because the concept of *Bildung* made a common point of
departure with Germans unnecessary that it had played such a
major role in the process of Jewish emancipation. The children of
the ghetto could enter German culture ignoring the burden of their
past. For Buber, the point of departure was the *Volk,* but his Jewish
Volk, however similar to the German, was neither narrow nor
chauvinist and tolerated a wide variety of opinions. Moreover, the
Volk was only a stepping-stone toward a common humanity.[54]
Thus, despite his point of departure, Buber's point of arrival was
similar to that advocated in Lessing's *Nathan the Wise.* For all of
his advocacy of a national mystique, Buber had absorbed much of
the older *Bildung* and Enlightenment.

Martin Buber's German-Jewish tradition had a future in the
Zionist movement, while the German-Jewish tradition which has
concerned us was beyond religion or nationalism. Yet they shared
a common substance, and important figures moved easily between
the two traditions—men such as Gustav Landauer, a socialist and
individualist who found a home in the Jewish people, [55] and Gershom Scholem, who combined an interest in Jewish mysticism
with the ideal of *Bildung* and the constant exercise of a critical
mind. The connections between these two traditions need further
investigation.

Thus one German-Jewish tradition did exist which, whatever
its specific Jewish components, also made use of German popular
culture—the revolutionary and utopian component, combined
with its emphasis on faith and its concern with the totality of life.
The other tradition, however, was not only alienated from popular
culture as a faith but in addition failed to understand the revolutionary and utopian components of popular culture. Martin Buber

used his mysticism as a mainspring for Zionist political action, while for Ludwig and Zweig the primacy of culture continued to preclude politics.

If Martin Buber narrowed the vision held by Zweig and Ludwig, he still kept the idea of a common humanity firmly in view. Yet there were some among German-Jewish intellectuals who wanted to shed the liberal culture for the sake of a *Volk*ish vision. Jakob Wassermann, a novelist as popular as Zweig and Ludwig during the years between the wars, provides a good example of such attitudes, and his eventual bitterness was that of an unrequited lover rather than reflecting loss of hope for the triumph of *Bildung* and humanity. Wassermann wanted to be a German writer, probing the German soul, wandering through the narrow and crooked streets of ancient provincial towns, analyzing the gnarled men and women who lived there. The image of the *Volk* was engraved on his soul, he wrote in 1915, while modernity threatened the mythical force of love for the fatherland and its customs.[56] Wasserman wrote the novel *Caspar Hauser* (1908) in order to establish his credibility as a German writer.[57] It is the story of a youth straight out of a fairy tale, as he puts it, who appears, apparently from nowhere, in a little town; the youth speaks with the pure voice of nature, believing all men to be good and beautiful. As a "myth come to life," Caspar Hauser is persecuted by men and women who cannot tolerate innocence and beauty, who must constantly probe and question, and who attempt to catch him in their web of official rules and regulations.[58] Eventually he is murdered by a stranger, and while Wassermann implies that Caspar Hauser was a prince, his life is shrouded in mystery. The dark forces of the soul are defeated by shallow reality. Surely Wassermann is the counterpoint to the rational and optimistic German-Jewish tradition.

There was no lightness of touch in Wassermann's works; he was always in earnest, preoccupied with serious matters. His most famous novel, *Gänsemännchen (Gooseman,* 1915), is filled with characters at the brink of insanity from their compulsive examination of their own and other people's souls. Suffering is total, corresponding to the small and tortuous alleys of the old provincial town where the action takes place. But the end is romantic and happy—the hero, a musician, surrounded by devoted students, has attained harmony through his music, transcending his emotional agony and material deprivations.

Wassermann was troubled by his Jewishness and by his fellow Jews. Not only were Jews the "Jacobins of our times," as he wrote in his autobiography, but he hated the rootless Jews—the *Kulturjuden,* as he called them [59]—precisely those Jews who are our main concern. He himself lacked all Jewish education and felt no religious or national solidarity with his fellow Jews, a characteristic he shared with many of those he condemned. His Jewishness also depended upon an inner substance for which he searched diligently until he found it in a so-called synthesis between a vague Jewish "orientalism" and the German soul. The supposed German reality is measured against this ideal in *Mein Weg als Deutcher und Jude* (*My Life as German and as Jew,* 1921), a book quite wrongly taken as typical of German Jewry.

The synthesis failed. *Caspar Hauser* was not recognized as the great German novel of its time, and in *My Life as German and as Jew* Wassermann struck out against the German hatred of Jews which he blamed for that failure. He contrasted such hatred not to the tolerance and rationality of France, as did so many German-Jewish intellectuals, but to the supposed liberality of postwar Austria—a bizarre contrast which reflects his paranoia as a German writer.[60] Jews themselves had to bear much of the blame for Jew-hatred because of their "recognizable Jewish traits"—instability, materialism, and cunning.[61] Wassermann moved easily from probing people's souls to accepting their stereotypes. This preoccupation with the German soul, the so-called mysteries which coursed underneath the superficialities of life, was apt to encourage the use of obvious symbolism. Thus, when the hero of *Gänsemännchen* decides to marry, a bat flies into the window, portending the time when his future wife will burn all his music.

Wassermann's books are forgotten, yet at the time he was considered the equal of Thomas Mann as one of Germany's most famous writers. It is easy to see why his fame has vanished—his books were carried on a wave of *Volk*ish introspection. Wassermann's pessimism about his particular German-Jewish symbiosis was misplaced; he was only too German a writer. Typically, Stefan Zweig criticized Wassermann for his inwardness, his lack of open-mindedness to the rest of the world.[62] Yet Zweig was too harsh a critic, for in spite of his *Volk*ish ideal, Wassermann believed that his narrow focus would not preclude a wider vision of humanity. Although the image of the *Volk* was supposedly engraved on everyone's soul, in Wassermann's essays and speeches he called for a "true humanism" based upon love for all men.[63] Commitment to one's own *Volk* was a means of overcoming one's selfishness, of taking the first step toward a true humanity.[64] Yet this theme is muted in his novels, where the individual remains firmly embedded in the German *Volk*.[65] Thus Wasserman was also touched by a larger vision of self-fulfillment, standing however shakily, within the German-Jewish intellectual tradition.

Wassermann's attempt to reach out to the German people was different from that of Berthold Auerbach, Emil Ludwig, or Stefan Zweig. They had idealized the German people by transforming them into a self-designed image of the cosmopolitan and cultured middle class. Wassermann was closer to the mystical and apocalyptic trend of German popular culture, although he did not share its sometimes aggressive intent or its revolutionary message. Wassermann, to a limited extent, and Buber, decisively, rejected German popular culture's exclusive claim to truth and dominance. Indeed, although Wassermann supported the Weimar Republic, unlike Zweig or Ludwig, he was not merely opposed to revolutionary violence but hostile to all political radicalism—a hostility based on the participation of so many Jews in the German revolution after the war. He considered them to be opportunists who had wasted their lives in futile opposition—fanatics who had become mere human skeletons.[66] Wassermann feared and abhorred the rootlessness he thought that Jewish revolutionaries symbolized because he considered it an obstacle to his own acceptance as a German writer. Here Wassermann departed from the tradition of *Bildung* and Enlightenment, which had made Ludwig and Zweig take a more sympathetic stand towards peaceful revolution.

And yet the Germanic commitment of Wassermann, like Buber's belief in a Jewish *Volk*, although closely related to trends in German popular culture, refused to acknowledge its logical political implications. Both men accepted a nineteenth-century patriotism rather than the postwar nationalism which was increasingly monopolized by the political right. In addition, however, concern for all humanity played a role in their thought—central in Buber's Zionism, peripheral to Wassermann's identification with Germany. Buber's ties to the mainstream of the German-Jewish tradition were stronger than Wassermann's. Such attitudes, especially the concept of nationalism as patriotism, were rapidly becoming archaic during their own lifetime. Is it that the outsider who has become an insider—the newly emancipated—can never shed the tradition of his emancipation? Despite his undoubted attraction to popular culture, he cannot share its faith, because he does not share the historical past so essential to its very being. Those who found consolation in *Nathan the Wise* were, after all, on firmer ground than those Jews who attempted the plunge into German popular culture—not to elevate it, but in order to swim with the tide.

The failure of Zweig and Ludwig to make meaningful contact with popular culture sums up the position not just of those authors but of an articulate and influential segment of German Jewry. They continued to uphold ideals which had informed Jewish emancipation but which by this time no longer presented a usable past. Moreover, they were apt to mistake the German bourgeoisie for the German people, as this was all they really knew—a result of the successful emancipation of Jews into the German middle class. Yet by the post-World War I years, the Jewish middle class was becoming increasingly isolated from the main currents influencing the German middle class.

Emil Ludwig's biographies did not survive World War II, and only Zweig's novels, rather than his historical works, are being republished in our time. Zweig was no doubt a better writer; Ludwig's breathless style makes his books seem shallow, although both used the kind of hyperbole which is out of fashion today. The years which followed World War II encouraged instead the rediscovery of writers like Kafka, who wrote about existential situations which allow no clear-cut solutions. Moreover, historical writing had changed, and even popular works of history were better researched, less dependent on the decisive moment or the workings of a just fate. Yet Zweig did paint a memorable picture of the past in the one book which has outlasted his others, *Die Welt von Gestern* (*The World of Yesterday*, 1944), finished shortly before his death and published posthumously. In it he used a broad canvas rather than dramatizing history, and he relied on his own observation of people and events. Although it was supposed to be an autobiography, his shyness denied him the concentration on personal character which was typical of his biographies. Since Emil Ludwig could never transcend his own style, his autobiography does not differ from his other popular works.

Even so, the Jewish identity these writers sought to convey was not lost, like Wassermann's quest for rootedness. They were in the tradition of *Bildung* and Enlightenment, presenting an alternative to the narrowing cultural and political vision of their time. Their true importance derives from their effort to reach out to popular culture. Jews did become best-selling authors, and on that level they entered into a dialogue with the German people, even though it was a dialogue which missed its purpose.

In contrast to those writers concerned about maintaining a wide audience, other German-Jewish intellectuals attempted to counter the ever-present dangers to *Bildung* and the Enlightenment from within high culture. Some tried to remind Germans of these ideals by keeping alive the great writers of that age—Goethe, Schiller, and Lessing would recall for Germans the glory of their classical age. At the same time, others—academics or private scholars for the most part—sought to use scholarship and their intellectual authority as a weapon to stem the tide which threatened to engulf all rational and cultivated minds.

III

Intellectual Authority and Scholarship

MANY GERMAN JEWS had broken their ties with a specific Jewish tradition and yet did not intend to become Christians. The void between traditional Christianity and Judaism as a revealed religion was filled by the ideal of *Bildung*, which had prevailed among the German bourgeois during the period of Jewish emancipation. It provided a meaningful heritage for some of the most articulate and intellectual German Jews. Eventually, the belief in individualism and the potential of human reason was eroded as nationalism—a world of myth and symbol—attempted to take its place.

Many Jews refused to adopt this narrowing vision; the more the older concept of *Bildung* came under attack, the more easily it could be accepted as one's own Jewish substance. At a time when many Germans found a secular religion in nationalism, Jews also found a secular faith—in the older concept of *Bildung*, based on individualism and rationality. The system of thought that had served to further Jewish emancipation still seemed to provide the best hope for completing the process.

German-Jewish writers, journalists, and intellectuals typically believed that culture determined politics, a heritage from their process of assimilation. They gained no understanding of the imperatives of mass politics in the modern age—they were *Bildungsbürger* trying to be good citizens. How deep this commitment to *Bildung* ran among Jews will be seen in more detail in the activities of the Jewish cultural ghetto under the Nazis, the *Jüdische Kulturbund*. With great determination, it tried to further what it called the "true spirit of Germany" by staging Lessing's *Nathan the Wise* and plays by Goethe and Schiller. However, when some of its leaders attempted to introduce Hebrew or eastern European plays in translation, they were unable to generate widespread enthusiasm.[1]

German Jews constantly reaffirmed their perception of themselves as representatives of reason, enlightenment, and *Bildung*. They confronted the rightist and nationalist ideal of the "simple person unspoiled by intellectuality, pure of heart and filled with goodwill."[2] The ideal German of the political right was such a simple person, relying on instinct and emotion, provincial and narrow in outlook. After 1880, when an unprecedented new wave of anti-Semitism swept through the country, German Jews still hoped that the German classical tradition might triumph over evil and that, like Captain Alfred Dreyfus in France, German Jews would be rehabilitated—finally accepted into true citizenship. In fact, between 1900 and World War I, overt anti-Semitism declined once more in a spectacular manner. French anti-Semitism had been even more virulent than that in Germany at the *fin de siècle*,[3] but unlike France, Germany contained no proper antibodies against the neoromanticism and nationalism surging to the fore—no Cartesian or Enlightenment tradition cutting deep, no French revolutionary tradition to counter the threat in the long run.

German and Jewish *Bildungsbürger* tried to keep the German classics alive as one of the chief bulwarks against the predominance of feeling and instinct. Goethe, Schiller, Lessing, Herder, and Fichte were heroes for Jews and gentiles alike, mythical figures who served to define German culture. However, in order to bolster their own concept of culture, most Germans eventually began to define these classics differently from German Jews. Thus, for example, in the mainstream of German culture, Herder, who had been a man of the Enlightenment, was transformed into a prophet of nationalism, and even Goethe, who had failed to support the German wars of liberation against the French,[4] was considered a German patriot.

Fichte made such co-optation easy through his famous

speeches to the German nation, given in Berlin under Napoleonic occupation, with their strident nationalism and hatred of Jews. Yet it is characteristic of the manner in which many Jews continued to view these classics that the early German Zionists claimed Fichte as one of their ancestors, raising the cry, "We must become little Fichtes." The young Zionists influenced by Martin Buber read Fichte differently from most Germans. In *Reden an die deutsche Nation (Addresses to the German Nation,* 1807), they found not hatred and aggression but signposts of how personal ethics might be reinforced through national commitment.[5] Nationalism was an ethical imperative, a means of developing one's own personality. The Fichte they read was not the Fichte whom many Germans saw as the advocate of the state as the sole moral, ethical, and political authority. Hermann Cohen, the anti-Zionist, had a similar view. Fichte was the first, he wrote, to recognize the Old Testament ideal of a nation in the service of universal freedom.[6]

In their undrstanding of other classics as well, many Jews went back to the age in which these writers had lived and worked—a time in which nation, freedom, and individualism had been joined. German Zionists such as Robert Weltsch used the appeal to Fichte in order to caution against chauvinistic nationalism, not to further it. Apart from such Zionists, however, Fichte played a minor role for Jews compared to Lessing, Schiller, and Goethe.

Friedrich Schiller, in particular, was perceived as an advocate for cosmopolitanism and equality, a spokesman for humanitarian ideals. His exaltation of freedom served as a bridge to European culture, especially for Jews in eastern Europe, who could read him in Hebrew or Yiddish. In this context, Schiller played a greater role than Goethe as the prophet of freedom and equality—a poet who touched the emotions. Those longing for a secular *Bildung* in eastern Europe talked about "Schiller-Goethe," reversing the order in which they were usually listed.[7]

For German Jews, however, Goethe fulfilled an even more important function. His own prejudice against the Jews in the Frankfurt ghetto was forgotten, as was Schiller's crafty brigand Spiegelberg. Goethe's emphasis on individual freedom, his ambivalence toward all forms of nationalism, and, finally, his belief in *Bildung* seemed to foster Jewish assimilation. More important, unlike Schiller, Goethe was the embodiment of the ideal *Bildungsbürger* of the period of Jewish emancipation. Thus one of the most popular biographies of Goethe, that by Albert Bielschowsky, which sold some 80,000 copies between 1895 and 1912, called Goethe's "genuine humanity" the goal toward which all mankind must strive.[8] Goethe, although a genius, was said to exemplify normality; although his feelings were more intense and his thoughts deeper than those of his fellowmen, his language was restraint, as he rejected all extremes.[9] Bielschowsky, like so many Goethe biographers a Jew, saw in Goethe the representative of that bourgeoisie which had welcomed Jewish emancipation. "Until today Goethe is still . . . a subterranean influence," Bielschowsky wrote in 1893, "one knows of his existence, admires him now and then, but one is not willing to be elevated and inspired by him."[10] Goethe, the "normal" bourgeois of the classical period, was supposed to cure the bourgeoisie which had become infected with the extremes of nationalism and neoromanticism.

The fact that German Jews played a leading role in Goethe societies and wrote so many Goethe biographies documents the poet's importance to the integration of Jews into Germany. For example, Ludwig Geiger, the son of a famous rabbi active in the Jewish reform movement, founded the *Goethe Yearbook* in 1880, and in the mid-1920s, Jews were almost a majority in the Berlin Goethe society. [11] Here was a bridge toward acceptance through identification with Germany's cultural hero.

Because Goethe was being nationalized and romanticized, and thus in danger of being placed in the anti-Semitic pantheon, it seemed of great importance to German Jews to join Goethe and Heinrich Heine, the master who was likened to the sun in a cloudless sky.[12] Heine was the cynical and restless Jew who for anti-Semites symbolized the destruction of German values. The complex and largely hostile relationship between Goethe and Heine was transformed into one of respect and enduring friendship; Heine as the supposed disciple of Goethe became a metaphor for Jewish assimilation. The most famous German-Jewish writer, in his close association with the German sage, was tamed into the restraint and harmony which Goethe was thought to possess. When the worship of Goethe reached its greatest intensity in the Berlin salons presided over by Jewish women of culture, Rahel von Varnhagen—frustrated and unhappy, never accepted as a Jew, so she thought, in the world of German culture—wrote in 1808 that "he accompanies me throughout my life without fail . . . strong and healthy, he conveys a harmony which unhappy and torn asunder I could never attain by myself."[13]

A century later, for most Germans, Goethe no longer stood for such balance and harmony. For example, a school principal talking to his graduating class in 1903 described Goethe as a lover of nature and art, filled with faith in the German *Volk*.[14] To be sure, some Jews played their part in romanticizing Goethe; Friedrich Gundolf constructed a myth which called Goethe poetry become flesh.[15] Others, such as the Goethe enthusiast and Frankfurt rabbi, Nehemia Anton Nobel, one of the most charismatic among the German-Jewish religious leadership, stressed Goethe's serenity and his emotional life as an artist. Judaism and Goethe had much in common, Nobel preached in 1922—a serene world view and the belief that every religion was an artistic creation.[16] Judaism and *Bildung* were as inexorably linked in the twentieth century as they had been by rabbis preaching during the age of emancipation.

Lessing, as noted earlier, was destined to play a major role among German Jews. Berthold Auerbach rhymed that Goethe and Schiller borrowed their fire from Lessing's flame.[17] During the height of the Wilhelminian wave of anti-Semitism, Auerbach tried to gather subscriptions for a Lessing monument, a task which Gabriel Riesser had attempted unsuccessfully many years previously. The call to subscribe asked that the monument be built to remind present-day Germans of a nobler past.[18] While such a call may seem to us a touching and naive reply to the tide of nationalism and neoromanticism, we must remember that Wilhelminian Germany was the age of monuments. However, some made fun of "Goethemania," and others deplored the proliferation of monuments of all kinds—to poets, generals, and kings.[19] With the founding of a society to combat anti-Semitism in 1893, Jewish leaders took a more practical step to oppose the dangerous trends of the times. Love for the German classics was thought to provide a barrier of equal strength, though, to direct men back to an age of tolerance and reason.

Such uses of the classics did not leave a lasting or specific German-Jewish heritage. Others, however, followed the same path of *Bildung,* looking back to the same period of history but, instead of relying upon the classics, attempting to use their own scholarship to exorcise the irrational, to render it harmless by filtering it through the rational mind. Such scholars eventually left a more lasting heritage than those who had tried to influence popular culture or those who had appealed to the authority of the German classics. Their confrontation with the irrational forces of the age was destined to reinvigorate whole fields of study and to extend the boundaries of traditional disciplines, founding a new kind of cultural history.

Scholarship of this type rediscovered the importance of myth as determining the actions of men and society. The study of myths was transferred from anthropology, where it had played a leading role for some time, to the social sciences and the humanities. Myth was no longer confined to the thought of primitive man but was treated as a present concern, an enemy to be defeated and exorcised. These scholars considered the hunger for myth to be a threat to liberal values.

At the beginning of the twentieth century, a whole generation of German thinkers was in search of a mythology which would revive the suppressed emotions of men as a counterweight to cold reason. Such a mythology required thinking in visible and experiential categories which had always determined popular culture. Such thought was supposedly based on eternal truth—the substance of man which determined his wishes and drives. This substance was expressed through myths like those about the Germanic gods or the equally ancient Edda—myths which pointed to man's substance and gave him roots. Martin Buber shared these ideas, just as he had attempted to harness the thought of the German mystics to the Jewish revival. But while this mythology was rooted in the Jewish *Volk,* it expanded to manifest itself as a substance which was shared by all of humanity. Among the German political right, however, the mythology never expanded; the Germans alone were said to be in touch with the elemental forces of nature.[20] The mythology was brought to earth through the invocation of national symbols pointing to a history long past when the modern age had not yet crushed the Germanic soul. Millenarian and apocalyptic ideals played their part—the "German revolution" promised national salvation. The ancient Germans, medieval mystics, and racial memories were conjured up in order to fight a supposedly cosmopolitan, rational, and urban world.

Such is the background against which those dedicated to the older concept of *Bildung* attempted to exorcise myth—not only against the longing for a Third Reich in which the Germanic soul preserved through centuries of oppression would spring to life but also against the threat of rightist mass movements built on these foundations.

Sigmund Freud sought to give a rational analysis to personal myth against the background of the first large-scale anti-Semitic mass movement in central Europe. The fall of Vienna to Karl Lueger's anti-Semites in the election of 1895 was a stunning blow to liberal culture. Freud's commitment to a world of reason and his love for the German classics hardly need documentation. Freud harbored a formidable rationalist suspicion of enthusiasm and discounted all enthusiasms alike. He stood squarely in the tradition of the Enlightenment and what it had meant and still meant to many Jews, even though he lived in Vienna rather than Berlin. *Sulamith* had written in 1817 that man must grow in order to become an independent being, cultivating his reason in order to weaken the power of instinct; the parallel to the ego and the id seems obvious.[21] Of equal relevance for Freud's attack on myth was his attitude toward the tyranny of history. In the unconscious, he writes in *The Interpretation of Dreams* (1900), nothing can be brought to an end, nothing is past and done with. It is the task of psychotherapy to make it possible for the unconscious processes to be finally dealt with and forgotten.[22] If a wish to be free from the fate of his fellow Jews was present in *Die Traumdeutung (The Interpretation of Dreams)*, as has been argued,[23] then Freud's ambivalence toward history could be seen as putting an end to this separate fate—the history which Jews could not share with Germans or German Austrians.

Freud was interested in the past, as his analysis of Michelangelo shows, but this was a commitment to history as progress from animism through religion to science and culture—a typically liberal view of history. The ideals of rationalism, progress, and humanity made up Freud's Jewish substance, as they had informed the Jewishness of Auerbach and Zweig.[24] The autonomy of the individual was pitted against the masses, and Freud's view of the masses was no different from that of the other *Bildungsbürger* we have discussed. His *Massenpsychologie und Ich-Analyse* (*Group Psychology and the Analysis of the Ego*, 1921) was meant to demonstrate how the rational individual sinks into barbarism under the compulsion of group life.[25]

The discovery of psychoanalysis was set in part within the cultural tradition which has concerned us and seems to have sprung from a drive to restore a world lost in the noise of modern mass politics and industrial society. The modern psychoanalytic movement at first had the appearance of a Jewish sect, as the marginality of Jews in German-Austrian society was compounded by the fact that psychoanalysts were outsiders in the medical profession as well. Freud was quite aware of this double outsider status; it served, together with the political events in Vienna, to make him a self-conscious and self-questioning Jew. Freud and his circle of friends and correspondents were preoccupied with the battle to maintain reason and *Bildung*. Self-dignity and mutual support were regarded by some of these intellectuals as part of their Jewish substance.[26] Thus the writer Arnold Zweig welcomed a letter from Freud as a greeting from the "heart of the creative zone, from warmth and goodness of heart, and from the great European tradition of reason."[27] Freud constantly sought to widen the circle of his disciples and admirers, and through his correspondence and friendships he became a part of a republic of letters which transcended any sectarianism. Typically, this larger circle was oriented toward culture; hardly any medical men were a part of this network of personal relationships. The rival psychoanalysts and sexologists—some, like Krafft-Ebing, much more famous than Freud—went their own way and all but ignored this Jewish sect, which for a time managed to influence those concerned with literature and the arts rather than the medical profession.

During the years between the wars, this republic of letters was comprised of intellectuals trying to stem the tide of irrationalism and authoritarianism, men who knew and wrote to each other across national boundaries. Romain Rolland, the indefatigable correspondent, played an important role in this republic, as did, among others, André Gide, Benedetto Croce, Thomas Mann, and Ortega y Gasset. A true dialogue took place between these men and Jews from German-speaking lands, such as Sigmund Freud,

Martin Buber, Emil Ludwig, and Stefan and Arnold Zweig. Many of these writers also appeared in journals edited by left-wing intellectuals during the Weimar Republic. This republic of letters championed the dignity of the individual—the cause of humanity against darkening times. It has not yet found its historian, but when its history is written, its part in furthering a Jewish-gentile dialogue must not be forgotten.

Of course, there were differences among these men. For example, Freud's relationship with Romain Rolland began fraternally after World War I but ended in friction when Rolland dismissed some of Freud's most basic psychoanalytic theories.[28] Reflecting popular prejudice in one of his biographies, Emil Ludwig attacked Freud for projecting onto the healthy the notions Freud gained by observing the sick. He accused Freud of equating neurotics with normal men.[29] His emphasis on normalcy reflected the fear of being thought abnormal—of departing from the standards set by bourgeois society; this fear was shared by Jews and gentiles alike. Ludwig was too shallow to recognize that Freud also shared this fear—that he wished to change neurotic behavior to conform to the standards of society even while he argued for less repression of the instincts within the limits of respectability.[30]

The members of this republic of letters were not alone in their exploration of myth as a way of exorcising the irrational. They were joined by scholars who spoke primarily to an academic rather than a lay audience. Aby Warburg might, at first glance, seem an unlikely subject for our study—a private scholar, withdrawn from politics, the author of a very few erudite articles of far-reaching importance for the field of Renaissance art. Warburg's life's work after 1902 was the expansion of his library, first affiliated with the new University of Hamburg. After his death, the Warburg Library, in exile from National Socialism, moved to London, to be known as the Warburg Institute. In both Hamburg and London, it gave a new impulse to cultural history. Much has been written about Warburg and his institute, emphasizing their contribution to the discipline of art history. His significance in continuing a tradition of German Jewry has generally been neglected.

Aby Warburg's work dealt with the persistence of the classical tradition in the Renaissance—what the classical world had meant to Renaissance artists. Symbols and images were said to be the means by which man communicated his emotions, fears, and hopes to others; each basic human attitude demanded a particular symbol or image.[31] Through an analysis of symbols and images, expressed in Renaissance painting by the movements of figures, Warburg gave a new and fresh interpretation to the influence of the classics on Renaissance art. Warburg's definition of images as based on myths and expressed in symbols reflects (perhaps unconsciously) an understanding of an age where the visual was becoming more important than the printed word—where images expressed the hopes, fears, and wishes of the semi-literate masses. Warburg feared the masses, and his analysis centered on myth and symbol in order to exorcise the irrational through understanding its function; he wanted to use the rational mind to cope with the irrational.

Warburg sought to demonstrate that a principle of order governed all phenomena. This principle was embodied in the classics. Warburg's disciple and collaborator, Gertrud Bing, wrote about his belief that "the worship of the classics had been commonplace for all men of culture *(gebildeten)* ever since the eighteenth century."[32] The ideal of *Bildung* prevailed once more. For Warburg, paganism meant surrender to the impulses of frenzy and fear, while the classics were seen through the eyes of Nietzsche as both Apollonian and demoniac. Thus classic inspiration could lead to unrest—the blowing hair and billowing dresses of some Renaissance painting—but would eventually induce restfulness.[33] Toward the end of his life (he died in 1929), Warburg saw the demoniac victorious more often than the Apollonian.[34] Like Freud, Warburg sided with reason against the dark side of the psyche. He considered it his duty to assist the struggle for enlightenment precisely because he knew the strength of the enemy.[35] Warburg was fascinated by astrology, and to the dualism between the Apollonian and the demoniac he added the one between magic and logic. Athens, he wrote, must always be saved from Alexandria.[36]

In his way, Warburg continued what the Enlightenment had attempted—to exorcise the irrational by comprehending it rationally. The ideal of *Bildung* is always present, reflected in the importance of the classics, essential for the cultivation of human self-consciousness through the ages. Warburg's was an *Aufklärer's* (enlightener's) prescription for life in a world threatened by irrationality. Indeed, Gertrud Bing states that Lessing's essay on the statue of Laocoon—that symbol of restraint and quiet greatness in the midst of pain—was a powerful influence on Warburg's youth and that he felt a deep obligation to the German Enlightenment.[37]

The urge toward totality marked among all of these intellectuals determined the arrangement of books in Warburg's famous library; books on philosophy were next to those on astrology, magic, and folklore, and sections on art were linked to literature, religion, and philosophy. Warburg thus implemented his belief that man's consciousness must not be torn apart through one-sidedness and exaggeration; it must be in balance, just as the world should be governed by reason. Surely Aby Warburg must be placed within the tradition of *Bildung;* like others, he attempted to fight a rearguard action against the narrowing vision of his time, but with different weapons. He had a clear vision of the irrational forces which seemed to dominate his life and times.

Warburg came from an orthodox Jewish home and broke with its traditions early in life. This break seemed necessary to him in order to realize his youthful intention to define the "typical character" of an enlightened and assimilated Jew. He intended to place himself on neutral ground, neither a Christian nor a traditional Jew; nevertheless, he considered his Jewishness a proud heritage.[38] His project of defining the Jew was never realized, but for him, as for other intellectuals, Jewishness was in fact identical with *Bildung,* because it exemplified the attitude toward life of the German bourgeoisie in its classical age.

Warburg always stressed the necessity of space for quiet reflection *(einen Raum der besonnenheit)* which would strengthen rationality.[39] But just as important as such space was scholarship itself—control over the human imagination through a meticulous examination of documents. Warburg's own essays are detailed examinations of evidence, filigree work in the tracing of classical influence. General statements are rare and must be pieced together from his approach to research and a few speeches of a more reflective nature. For Aby Warburg, scholarship was a way to maintain rationality in an increasingly complex and irrational world, a means of maintaining control in a world bordering on chaos—to warn, to exorcise, to encourage, never detached from the challenge of the times.[40]

Erwin Panofsky, one of the Warburg library's most famous collaborators (and like almost all of its early collaborators a Jew), emphasized this ordering function of scholarship. The objects which art history studies, he wrote, come into being through an irrational and subjective process, the art of creation, which the art historian must bring under control. The humanist must be suspicious of mere "art appreciation"; knowledge of classical languages, the historical method, and relevant documents is needed in order to truly understand a work of art—to integrate it into the structure of the rational mind.[41] The classics are crucial here as well; neither Warburg nor Panofsky had any use for the "nervous" baroque, unrestrained by the Apollonian. Moreover, as a believing Christian, Michelangelo had surrendered to medieval and Gothic prototypes. The classics signified the awakening of mankind from Christianity and the baroque to his *Bildung* and enlightenment.[42] Such an awakening was crucial to man's ability for self-cultivation.

The Warburg library's most prolific author, Ernst Cassirer, wanted to accomplish for philosophy what Warburg and Panofsky had attempted in art history—the imprisonment of irrational activity within a rational critique of culture. For Cassirer as well, symbols united human thought and existence through the structures of language, religion, myth, and art. Such a world was knowable by virtue of the systematizing tendencies of human reason.[43] Lecturing at the Warburg Institute in London in 1936, Cassirer proclaimed that the idea of liberty was basic to any philosophy of history or culture and that liberty was founded upon the autonomy of human reason.[44] But where Warburg had been pessimistic about the victory of human reason, Cassirer was optimistic, for he shared with Kant and Hegel a teleological view of humanity's progressive enlightenment. Man would increasingly come to understand the rational basis of his own existence and in this way gain control over the irrational. Myth, he wrote, feeds on a world of fantasy—in magic rites and religious ceremonies, man acts under the pressure of individual desire and violent social impulse. But once man begins to ask what such myths mean, the answers will lead him away from unconscious and instinctive life.[45] The similarity is startling between Cassirer's *Myth of the State* (1946) and the ideas of both Freud and Warburg, in spite of the fact that there was no close communication between the Warburg library and the psychoanalysts. They clearly shared a common German tradition which defined what they regarded as the substance of their Jewishness.

Why, then, did these men fail to apply their insights directly to the politics of their time? In exile from National Socialism, Cassirer did analyze the political myths of his time, calling them serpents which paralyzed their victims before attacking them. Modern man had not really surmounted the conditions of savage life, he said. Nor had mythical thought lost its potency, even if artistic, intellectual, and ethnic forces had checked its influence for a time.[46] Typically, political forces seemed to play no role in checking myth. Instead, culture provided the antidote, and while the preoccupation with myth and symbols in *The Myth of the State* comes tantalizingly close to an analysis of modern mass politics, its political implications were never explored. No more than any of the other German-Jewish intellectuals could Cassirer free himself from his bias toward *Bildung*.

The new impetus these scholars gave to art history, cultural history, and philosophy is still with us, although less in Europe than in England and the United States, where refugee scholars helped to assure continuity. Yet the kind of bourgeoisie they represented, with its reliance on the classics, has lost its relevance. To many intellectuals after World War II, living a balanced, rational, and steady life was of less consequence than questioning the very existence of their society—posing existential dilemmas. They wanted to retain the idealism of this German-Jewish tradition without its "stuffy" and complacent bourgeois heritage. The left-wing intellectuals of the Weimar Republic helped them to accomplish this feat.

IV

A Left-Wing Identity

THE GERMAN-JEWISH tradition reached its climax in a left-wing identity. The increasing difficulties in carrying on a German-Jewish dialogue were apparent in our analysis of those writers who wanted to break through their isolation in order to make contact with German popular culture. Others attempted to interact with German intellectual life through their scholarship, to use it in order to exorcise the irrational then pressing in on all sides. Such men were dedicated to the proposition that in the long run the senseless must make sense; this proposition guided their analysis of history and their attempt to explain myths and symbols. Much of German culture and politics no longer felt a need for rational explanations; instead, it withdrew into a world of faith. Those whose ideals we have discussed felt uneasy among believers—Jews or gentiles.[1] They had their own tradition of German culture, transmitted from the *Bildungsbürgertum* of an earlier age, and while they felt their growing isolation, they were rarely conscious of its effects or possible consequences. The left-wing intellectuals exemplified a powerful urge to integrate, to find their Jewish substance in German culture. Many of them were aware of their Jewishness but thought that through socialism they would arrive at the final point of transcendence beyond Judaism or Germanic roots.

The ideal of a common humanity which would abolish the

differences between all peoples was the final goal for all who had stood in this tradition; both *Bildung* and the Enlightenment were founded upon the autonomy of the individual, the potential of all men regardless of nationality or religion. This concept of humanity had been vague, and both Wilhelm von Humboldt and the philosophers of the Enlightenment were more concerned with how this ideal might be reached than with its special content. Later, it became a metaphor directed against dogmatism and intolerance, the expression of an individualism essential for the attainment of true culture. For men like Stefan Zweig, humanity meant transcendence of nation and religion, of all so-called artificial barriers among men, until, as he put it, pure friendship reigned.[2]

Left-wing intellectuals found that socialism made concrete the ideal of humanity by modernizing the manner in which such transcendence could be accomplished. The final victory of the working class and the abolition of existing property relationships would issue in the triumph of humanity, but such a victory would be meaningless unless it was based upon *Bildung* and the Enlightenment. As a result, theirs was a peculiar socialism, opposed by socialist orthodoxies and advocated during the Weimar Republic by men and women who were, for the most part, Jewish intellectuals.[3] To be sure, gentile intellectuals had also had a part in the creation of this socialism, but Jewish participation was much greater than gentile in this dialogue between Germans and Jews. For example, of the sixty-eight writers for the most important left-wing journal (*Die Weltbühne*) whose religious origins could be established, forty-two were of Jewish descent, two were half-Jews, and only twenty-four non-Jews.[4] The many German intellectuals who failed to remain liberals joined the orthodox right or left, where they could find shelter in a firm and simple ideology.

To be sure, many Jews also joined the orthodox left, and as members of the Social Democrats or of the Communist Party they never questioned the official dogmas, serving as good foot soldiers of the party and, at the beginning of the Weimar Republic, in leadership positions as well. Left-wing intellectuals were those who either could not bring themselves to join an established socialist party or, if they joined, proved troublesome, always questioning party dogma and policy. As noted elsewhere, the socialist parties felt a growing hostility toward intellectuals, and for some workers, to be a Jew was identical with being an intellectual.[5] Left-wing intellectuals saw themselves as the "conscience of the working class" and conceived of their mission as providing the yeast of socialism, keeping its structure flexible. Left-wing intellectuals saw socialism as a historical process rather than as a finished product. Their heritage became meaningful to the young men and women after World War II searching for a socialism untainted by the demands of politics or the struggle for power.

Not only did the socialism of the left-wing intellectuals give body to the vague ideals of humanity to which they paid allegiance, but open-mindedness to the new in German culture, characteristic of so many German Jews, helped them to move beyond liberalism. This would have been more difficult without the liberal heritage itself; the ideals of self-cultivation and the autonomy of man were central to their socialist ideology. There was an affinity between the Jewish bourgeoisie which supported the newest in the arts, placing themselves squarely on the side of the modernists, and their wayward socialist children, who wanted to overthrow the existing social and economic order. This affinity was based on shared ideals that the sons wanted to realize more completely than the fathers had.

The young socialists considered themselves Marxists—they advocated the class struggle, control over the means of production by the working class, and, finally, a classless society. They agreed wholeheartedly with the Marxist view of capitalism as draining away the surplus value produced by the workers and enslaving men through the fetishism of goods. They were less sure about the economic foundations of Marxist analysis and its political relativism—whether revolutionary tactics had to prevail until victory was won. Marxism, wrote Ernst Bloch, wants to preserve that ideal of humanity which the bourgeosie upheld in its classical period,[6] the time of Jewish emancipation. Marx himself believed that in the late eighteenth century the middle class had had a historical and progressive mission before it became an enemy in the class struggle. Some left-wing intellectuals, such as the young Georg Lukács, came to Marxism from a deep ethical rejection of the capitalist world and the desire to see oppressed peoples break with the old orders of society in order to shape their own destiny.[7]

The attempt to humanize Marxism dates back to the *fin de*

siècle but found its climax in the Weimar Republic as intellectuals attempted to reinvigorate the Hegelian roots of Marxism or to tie Marxism to Kant's categorical imperative. The Hegelian revival wanted to direct the attention of Marxism away from the world of things and to their human source. Those who wanted to emphasize the Hegelian dialectic tried to change the connection of the world of objects to man by altering how man perceived his world—how he comprehended the totality of life. They believed that man must understand the whole of his existence, the forces which shape it, and how he can attain his freedom. The liberal division of labor, of politics from life, was rejected, yet much of the substance of liberalism remained alive within the totality of true human consciousness.

The concern with culture remained uppermost, yet cultural phenomena were to be seen not in isolation from their social context or solely as products of class struggle, but mediated by the totality of life, including thought, politics, economics, and artistic creation. Orthodox Marxists were mistaken in deriving cultural phenomena solely from their substructural socioeconomic base. Nevertheless, for Hegelian Marxists such as Max Horkheimer and Theodor Adorno, the class struggle was not abolished but extended in dimension. The conflict between the old society and that about to be born was not merely a struggle for control over the means of production but informed all aspects of life.[8] Culture was given relatively greater weight than the means of production—modern mass culture, based upon the fetishism of goods through advertising or upon the manipulation of popular taste as an opiate for the masses (such as jazz, for Adorno), prevented true consciousness, the grasping of the totality of life. Moreover, further departing from the prevailing Marxist orthodoxy, the Hegelian dialectic was seen as open-ended (as indeed it had been for the young Hegel)—one that was interested, like *Bildung,* in the process rather than in the product of the struggle—and therefore refused to acknowledge the Soviet Union as the paradigm of the new society.

Many Hegelian socialists showed a bias in favor of aesthetics; Lukács's preoccupation with literature and Adorno's with music are good examples. The importance of aesthetics in *Bildung* is accepted even though the self-cultivation of man is not dependent solely on his own volition but also on social reality. However, in spite of the attempt to balance individuality with social reality, it is man who must act, as, for example, Lukács tells us, providing he understands the totality of his existence and is not lost in this world.[9]

Man must be freed from domination—that was the message of the so-called Frankfurt school, the Institute for Social Research established in 1923 at the newly founded University of Frankfurt, which attained its fame from 1930 onward under the leadership of Max Horkheimer and Theodor Adorno. The root of all evil was not merely the structure of social relationships but, above all, the tyranny of oppressive systems of thought and culture over the minds of men.[10] Emphasis was placed upon human cognition; only "true consciousness" could free itself from the contemporary network of domination designed to induce false consciousness. The term "mediation" is important here, for it was the mind of man which mediated between the individual and his comprehension of social reality. As the mind grew in self-consciousness, man would come to understand this reality better and would want to be part of the dialectic of change—facilitating the process by which the existing order would be transcended. The obstacles to such comprehension, and therefore to a revolutionary commitment, were the inducements offered by contemporary culture, which had been co-opted by capitalism and, corrupted by the system, had lost the liberating function it had possessed in the age of Goethe and Schiller. The capitalist system had destroyed all that was genuine, whether the human substance or culture; thus, for example, Adorno and Walter Benjamin (for a short time a member of the Institute) were preoccupied with art in an age of mechanical reproduction. The domination of systems over the minds of men made it impossible for men to mediate between their own needs and those of society.[11]

Despite the rejection of liberalism, a considerable amount of the concept of *Bildung* was assimilated in this emphasis upon the cultivation of the mind. Aesthetic perceptions occupied the same central place in this socialism that they had occupied in the concept of *Bildung*. Appreciation of the genuinely beautiful was an integral part of the true consciousness that would advance the dialectical process in order to transcend the present. All of these scholars were interested in the classics and classical beauty, although none of them thought that classical concepts provided a perfect model for the present or the future; socialism, like history and the original concept of *Bildung*, was a process, a striving for perfection not yet attained.

The primacy of culture entailed the primacy of theory, thus the term "critical theory" is often used to describe the ideology of the Frankfurt school. Barry Kātz has written that the so-called critical theory placed its hope for human liberation not in the misery of industrial workers but in some past ideals which remained true. The theorists of the Frankfurt school were sharply critical of the Enlightenment, accusing it of constructing a system of domination which equated mathematical abstractions with human thought. Yet they insisted on the use of the critical mind, itself an Enlightenment legacy, as the key ingredient in preparing the "leap into a totally other world."[12]

The search for transcendence—the attempt to understand the material world without being subordinated to its dictates—motivated most of the German-Jewish intellectuals we have discussed. For them, the search for transcendence was essential for an ideal social and political integration on the basis of a shared humanity. But for these socialists, conscious "alienation" from the present was a precondition for the "true consciousness" on which a better future could be built. Only by standing apart could men understand society in its entirety and begin the work for change. Thus outsiderdom itself became a necessary prerequisite for transcendence. Neither the Jewish nor the gentile bourgeoisie of the eighteenth-century Enlightenment would have understood such an idea; Jewish emancipation was supposed to be a denial of outsiderdom, not its affirmation.

The Hegelian revival of Marxism stressed not only mediation, true rather than false consciousness, and the aesthetic but also the open-endedness of history—its revolutionary potential. The Hegelian socialists wanted to revolutionize society, even though in later exile from Nazi Germany they disclaimed such an intention. To them, history was a process through which man worked to throw off domination by understanding the totality of his existence. Thus the fossilized structure of Marxism was pried open, leading to a vision of a future which might be never-ending, where man would strive ever upward to a final liberation. The avant-garde of this revolution were no longer the proletariat but a kind of *Bildungsbürger*—rational, informed, adept at theorizing, and with finely tuned aesthetic sensibilities. The importance given to music and literature, in particular, as necessary to the attainment of true consciousness seems startling. Interestingly, the strong emphasis on reason indicates French inspiration, as it did for the editors of the liberal press and men such as Zweig and Ludwig; according to Horkheimer and Adorno, "Humanity has always been more at home in France than elsewhere."[13]

The concerns which had been central to the German-Jewish tradition were integrated into a revolutionary theory. The members of the Institute for Social Research were apt to deny that their Jewishness played any part in their lives, a denial that had its source in their socialism. Martin Jay was correct when he wrote that the manifest intellectual context of Judaism—using a definition of Judaism as either a religion or based on specific and ancient Jewish traditions—played no part in their lives.[14] But their Judaism was very much present if defined as a German-Jewish identity which was becoming increasingly Jewish as most Germans repudiated it.

Their Jewishness played another role as well, one attuned to the concept of alienation in critical theory—they were outsiders in German university life, just as they were outsiders as far as the established socialist parties were concerned. The scholars of the Frankfurt school were conscious of their position, and although they asserted that Judaism played no role in their lives, they shared with other left-wing intellectuals the belief that Weimar Germany had to undergo massive transformation if anti-Semitism was to end. This conviction was clearly an important factor which, as Istvan Deak tells us, led many Jews to become left-wing intellectuals.[15] Max Horkheimer's own growing concern with the German hatred of Jews, which burst into the open in his old age, may well have been simmering throughout much of his life. We cannot examine in detail the attitudes of the leading members of the Frankfurt school toward anti-Semitism and their Jewish origins—Benjamin's flirtation with Judaism is well known, while Adorno, only half-Jewish, was much less concerned. Whatever their individual concerns were, the Frankfurt school as a whole is a part of the German-Jewish tradition of *Bildung* and Enlightenment and brought this tradition to the socialist movement. Placing such socialists in the German-Jewish tradition is not meant to deny the obvious influence of Marx, Hegel, and others on their thought, but the roots of this unorthodox socialism lie in large measure within the peculiar nature and evolution of a German-Jewish identity.

The ideals of the Frankfurt school were lasting ones. The methods of analysis—the Hegelian concept of mediation between the individual and society and the nature of human consciousness—were important, but the interrelationship between totality and freedom was even more so. The absence of commitment to a fixed class base was destined to appeal to those disillusioned with the proletariat; so was the attempt to break with the religion of industrial progress. The worship of industrial progress had come to prevail within Marxism, as in society as a whole—the laws of industrial production would lead to the victory of the proletariat. Such Marxism seemed to encourage the dehumanization of society, which these socialists and their intellectual heirs deplored. Hegelian socialism led back to the centrality of man himself—his mind and its cultivation—and thus served to humanize Marxism, so they thought, without denying the pressing need for revolution.[16] The New Left of the 1960s also criticized the way in which human life was transformed by modern capitalist society into things, marketable goods, or numbers.[17] Although they took this criticism from the early work of Lukács rather than from the Frankfurt school, the thrust of the young Hungarian activist intellectual and the German academics was much the same. The cultural emphasis of the Frankfurt school as basic to an understanding of the totality of life also had profound meaning to a generation of bourgeois youth in Europe and the United States in the 1960s—no longer Jews but mostly gentiles, children of prosperity yet discontent.

Herbert Marcuse, at one time a member of the Institute for Social Research, was instrumental in transmitting these ideas to later generations. His *One-Dimensional Man* (1964) concentrated on the humanist foundation of socialism as he castigated both capitalism and Bolshevism. A former student member of the New Left in the United States has described what it meant to realize for the first time that exploitation was not confined to physical or economic suffering[18] but included alienation from one's very humanity, an alienation symbolized by modern mass culture. The emphasis on domination was once more present as Marcuse contended that high culture did not simply deteriorate into mass culture but that two-dimensional culture became one-dimensional culture through its co-optation by the establishment.[19] Karl Marx's critique of the fetishism of goods was adapted to a theory which, while not denying the reality of class struggle, emphasized the importance of human consciousness. Marcuse stated that true consciousness must take up the fight against one-dimensional man, the co-optation by a restrictive society of all that was noble—tolerance and learning, literature and art.

Bourgeois society had corrupted the critical mind through co-optation, integrating it into a system of domination; so ran one of the principal theories of the New Left in Europe and the United States, continuing the thought not of orthodox Marxists but of these earlier left-wing intellectuals. Those who opposed one-dimensional man must now come to the rescue; the rescuers were not the proletariat, lacking consciousness but, above all, university students and the intelligentsia, who were not yet part of the establishment and were therefore freely able to exercise their reason—men and women of *Bildung*. The "outsider" was assigned his task, very similar to the one that Kantian socialists gave themselves and that others assigned to the so-called free-floating intelligentsia. The German-Jewish tradition had reached a decisive point—the freedom of the individual from all domination could be accomplished only by those who had internalized the tradition of self-cultivation, rationalism, and enlightenment. The bourgeois dimension of the age of emancipation had to be liquidated but its ideological substance preserved.

The Frankfurt school did its work in the shadow of National Socialism, making opposition to bourgeois society, as they perceived it, not only easier but a duty. Similarly, Marcuse saw liberalism as leading into fascism,[20] and the New Left in the 1960s invented a fascist menace in order to bring about the end of bourgeois society. In reality, however, they shared the ideological roots of liberalism, even though the liberalism of the classical period had changed. The substance of this liberalism became part of the German-Jewish tradition, much of it funneled through the concept of *Bildung,* and it was this kind of liberalism which opened up Marxist orthodoxy, just as it had opened up religious and cultural orthodoxy earlier. Our analysis of the German-Jewish heritage demonstrates this continuity—the constant, at times subterranean, workings of a Jewish substance as it had been defined from the beginning of Jewish emancipation.

The Kantian socialists in the Weimar Republic, also Jews for the most part, traveled a similar road, although instead of concentrating on the dialectical progress of history or the mediation between consciousness and society, they sought in a straightforward fashion to inject the categorical imperative into Marxism—an ethical standard which must determine all revolutionary action. The attraction of Kant for so many Jewish thinkers was in large part based on his cosmopolitan humanism and his emphasis on a critical mind informed by reason.[21] Kant expressed a moral ideal of *Bildung* which young left-wing intellectuals wanted to modernize by linking it to the insights of Marx. Their contention was that if Marx had drawn his context from Kant rather than from Hegel, his doctrine would not have been corrupted through tactics and discipline; one domination would not have succeeded another. Men must never be the means but rather the end of all striving, as the categorical imperative demanded. Kurt Eisner, later to lead the Munich revolution of 1918, wrote in his essay on "Marx and Kant" (1904) that Kant's ethic provided the living context which must determine human action taking place in history.[22] Like other Kantian socialists, Eisner did not negate the class struggle but put forward the standard by which it must be judged. The vision of a just society called for the abolition of capitalism. The original manifest of the *Weltbühne* (1918), the favorite journal of the left-wing intellectuals, demanded economic change but also asserted that the eternal imperative of justice and freedom must prevail during the struggle as well as in victory.[23]

Intellectuals had an important function in the Kantian scheme as well—they were the conscience of the working class and were to keep the ideal of the revolution unsullied until the final victory. During the revolutionary crisis of 1918, *Die Weltbühne* called for the formation of a "council of the wise" composed of those who had the proper ethical power of will. The "cultured" were to be the "true invisible church." Some intellectuals made an attempt to form such a council, but the workers' movement felt no need for the service of these intellectuals; indeed, both the Communists and the Social Democrats did their best to discipline or expel them.[24] The vagueness of the ethical ideal is evident; so is the commitment to an absolute, without the tempering influence of the Hegelian dialectic. Both the Kantian scheme and the Hegelian revival called for a new humanism which, while based upon *Bildung* and the Enlightenment, went beyond German liberalism and its increasingly narrow vision. What so many German Jews had considered their Jewish substance was preserved and extended.

The connection between Jewishness and the optimism of the Enlightenment continued full-blown in the philosophy of such men. However, especially in the advocacy of Kantian socialism, Jews were joined by gentiles; thus the book most often cited which derived from this view of man and society was not written by a Jew, although it symbolized the world view of many Jewish socialists. Leonhard Frank's *Man Is Good* (*Der Mensch ist gut*, 1919) activates the categorical imperative residing within every member of the so-called masses through the shrieks of a mother who has lost her son in the war and a waiter running through the streets, calling for an end to the conflict. The masses form an endless silent procession of sisters and brothers, marching toward the goal they all carry in their hearts—their wish to express love for all humanity despite the ruins of war. They march into a new society of truth, freedom, and love.[25] This triumph of humanity over death is based on a belief in the goodness of man, in his enlightened substance, which needs only to be awakened in order to transform society.

Frank, writing as a pacifist under the impact of war, was vague about the nature of this new society. Such vagueness is typical of much of Kantian socialism, although some, such as Kurt Eisner, wanted to create a government with shared power between soldiers and workers' councils and an elected parliament, and others suggested a form of welfare capitalism.[26] All Kantian socialists agreed, however, that the use of force and political tactics to bring about the revolution would corrupt the revolution itself and therefore had to be rejected.

Kantian socialism had some influence on later generations, but it was minor compared with the Hegelian revival of Marxism. Nevertheless, men such as Eisner, Ernst Toller, and the novelist

Lion Feuchtwanger, who, at one time or another, found Kantian socialism a congenial theory, were important Jewish left-wing intellectuals, not to be forgotten even after World War II.[27] The Jewish substance of the Kantian left-wing intellectuals is more elusive than that of the Hegelian socialists, although men such as Eisner and Toller were quite aware of their Jewishness. They shared the ethical idealism that was so strong in left-wing intellectuals—the urge to emancipate contemporary society from all that was fragmented and divisive. The "leap into freedom" of the Kantian socialists was necessary because the human substance demanded it, not because of a new self-consciousness brought about through self-cultivation, learning, and the development of aesthetic sensibilities. The Enlightenment was more important for Kantian socialists than *Bildung*. Still, they subordinated the class struggle to an ethical individualism—the sole technique for revolution.

The Jewishness of these left-wing intellectuals, from whatever school of socialist thought, was best expressed by the young Walter Benjamin, consciously seeking to define his own brand of Judaism. Benjamin, barely out of school at the age of twenty, rejoiced in his newly discovered Jewish identity. Jewish intellectuals, he wrote in 1912, provide the principal support and dynamic for true culture, which in this case included not only literature and art but also socialism and the women's emancipation movement. Among Jewish intellectuals, he continued, writers were in the vanguard of change; here the otherwise much maligned *Literatenjuden*—Jews as men of letters—took a central role in creating alternatives to the existing order.[28] Jewishness became a metaphor for the critical mind and for *Bildung;* it is through the study of Goethe, he repeats, that the nature of Jewishness is fully revealed.[29] This definition of Jewishness summarized in an almost uncanny manner the Jewish substance we have endeavored to trace—here not as an idealization of bourgeois society but as an alternative to the present.

Benjamin's Jewishness was in essence identical with that of the socialists we have discussed. The Frankfurt school sought his collaboration and after his death in 1941 published a memorial volume to secure for him the recognition denied during his life.[30] Yet Adorno, for one, disapproved of Benjamin's preoccupation with

Jewish thought, which for a time, under the influence of his close friend Gershom Scholem, seemed to shift Benjamin's early definition of Jewishness toward a sporadic interest in cabala and Zionism.[31] Nevertheless, Benjamin never departed far from the literature which he had defined as his Jewish substance. Gershom Scholem remembered that it was Benjamin's study of Goethe and Hölderlin and his translation of Baudelaire and Proust into German that led him to express a wish to know Hebrew in order to unravel the problems he had encountered in these activities.[32] Nothing much came of Benjamin's newly found interest, but it was not surprising that the road to a knowledge of Hebrew and to Zionism passed through the study of German culture.[33] A similar example was Buber's Hassidim, with their close ties to German mysticism.

Jewish socialist intellectuals were the prime targets of Social Democratic and Communist campaigns against intellectuals. August Bebel, the socialist leader who stood in the vanguard of the fight against anti-Semitism in Wilhelminian Germany, called Jewish socialists brilliant but pushy, difficult to subject to party discipline.[34] This attitude became rooted in orthodox socialism, and indeed the kind of socialism we have discussed did challenge orthodoxy, because it gave intellectuals a decisive role in the class struggle. The "outsider" wanted to become the "insider" in socialist thought as well—to find his roots in the working class, although the workers' movement continued to reject left-wing intellectuals. Just as the Jewish bourgeoisie was increasingly isolated within the German middle class, Jewish left-wing intellectuals were isolated within the workers' movement. Of course, anti-Semitism played a part in that isolation, especially within the Communist Party. The kind of socialism that Jewish intellectuals adopted was an equally important factor; neither socialist parties nor the workers' movement could accept the contention that theory must dominate practice. The workers' movement and the socialist parties stood in the midst of the political and social struggle, and it is no coincidence that the heirs of such left-wing intellectuals were idealistic and utopian middle-class university students and professors.

These Weimar intellectuals, with their theoretical and cultural preoccupations, were often unable to deal with the urgent political demands made on them; for example, when it came time to choose a presidential candidate for the elections of 1932, *Die Weltbühne,* after much soul-searching, recommended the Communist candidate, Ernst Thälmann—representing the very orthodoxy that the left-wing intellectuals had fought so bitterly.[35] Left-wing intellectuals such as the novelist Lion Feuchtwanger, in exile from Nazi Germany, may have had a better excuse for their flirtations with bolshevism, for the Soviet Union seemed to be the only nation committed to fighting fascism in the 1930s. Under Communist Party pressure, Georg Lukács repudiated his earlier writings. He believed that staying in the Communist Party meant keeping in touch with the masses and thus avoiding the political isolation of his fellow left-wing intellectuals.[36] The members of the Frankfurt school, such as Horkheimer and Adorno, never descended from their political aloofness into the arena of daily politics; Adorno despised popular culture and contemporary mass movements.[37]

The left-wing intellectuals were isolated not only from the reality of German politics and the dominant culture but also from their fellow Jews, however much they shared many of their liberal ideas. After 1918, they were repeatedly attacked as radicals who endangered all that Jews had managed to accomplish in Germany. Good reason existed for such attacks—Jews were highly visible in many of the postwar revolutions, not only in Bolshevik Russia but also in Budapest, Munich, and Berlin. That these Jews were for the most part Bolsheviks and not left-wing intellectuals made no difference to the popular perception. Indeed, only recently have historians begun to see the profound differences between the first stage of the Bavarian revolution, under Kurt Eisner, and its second, Bolshevik stage, under Eugen Leviné and others. To be sure, it is easy to see why Jews became Bolsheviks in eastern Europe, where their oppression had been harsh; the left-wing intellectuals, however, with their scruples about the use of force and their commitment to theory, stood at the other end of the spectrum in revolutionary Europe.

Anti-Semites and racists hammered home the lesson the revolutions were supposed to teach all Germans—Jews were Bolsheviks and anti-national. During the postwar crisis, belief in Jewish conspiracies and subversive activity was not just a curious notion held by professed haters of Jews; in 1918, even Winston Churchill associated Jews with the Bolshevik conspiracy.[38] It is no surprise, then, that left-wing activity was deplored by most Jews. The Jewish establishment had long been suspicious of Social Democrats; as noted earlier, at the beginning of the twentieth century, Jews had continued to support the liberals who flirted with anti-Semitism, rather than the Social Democrats, who proved to be their true friends.[39] Yet the left-wing intellectuals troubled Jews on a deeper level as well.

In *My Life as German and as Jew,* written just after the high tide of Jewish involvement in revolutionary activity, Jakob Wassermann asked why political radicalism sprang from a Judaism rooted in ancient and sacred traditions. He professed not to know the answer, partly because he failed to realize that to many Jews Socialists drew on the tradition of *Bildung* and the Enlightenment rather than on older, specifically Jewish traditions. Wassermann went on to characterize those attracted to left-wing radicalism as the uprooted, the professional "nay-sayers."[40] They were the "outsiders," who could not find stability in middle-class life. Left-wing intellectuals challenged German Jewry's assimilation into the German bourgeoisie. They threatened the close link between *Bildung* and the middle class which had existed since the creation of the concept. The middle-class way of life, including middle-class morals and manners, was considered an integral part of being cultured, *gebildet;* the Jews had been emancipated simultaneously into the age of *Bildung* and middle-class respectability.[41] Narrowing the horizon of *Bildung* did not change this way of life; indeed, it reinforced it.

Just as Jews clung to the older concept of *Bildung,* they clung to a middle-class way of life which continued to signify respectability. Ismar Schorsch has demonstrated how Moritz Oppenheim's scenes of pious Jewish family life, immensely popular among German Jews, mimicked German middle-class *Gemütlichkeit* even when they were set in the ghetto before emancipation.[42] Nor was it coincidental that Georg Hermann in his *Jettchen Gebert* (1906), required reading for young Jewish girls, praised the tranquil and steady life of the middle class. The left-wing Jewish intellectuals disrupted this life and thus threatened one of the principal pillars of Jewish emancipation. Socialist emphasis on grasping the totality of life challenged the bourgeois divisions of labor at the workplace and in everyday life. The left-wing intellectuals were accused of politicizing all aspects of life (an accusation leveled against the New Left in the 1960s as well).

Many German Jews in their own attitudes demonstrated a compartmentalization of life. They supported the avant-garde and sided with the modern in arts and letters, but they never extended these attitudes into social behavior or radical politics; the fabric of middle-class life was never tested. Moreover, in spite of their broader definition of *Bildung,* most German Jews agreed with the majority of the cultured bourgeoisie that citizenship meant respect for legitimate political authority, "which knows best." German Jews or Germans, the "little men" or the wealthy, were apt to follow Kant's precepts that a law was a law and that there can be no exceptions. The cultural and the political were two different worlds, and Jewish emancipation was a decisively cultural emancipation.

The middle class was successful in meeting all challenges to its way of life and survived unbroken even beyond World War II. When discontent flared once more among the sons and daughters of this bourgeoisie in the 1960s, many of the New Left, in Europe and the United States, adopted the Weimar left-wing intellectuals as their model. This heritage of the left-wing intellectuals can be briefly summarized, although with the splintering and proliferation of the New Left, many different influences came into play. The humanizing of Marxism had great appeal—it allowed emphasis on the centrality of the individual in the revolutionary process and the need for self-cultivation in order to understand the totality of existence. The quest for totality was pitted against the fragmentation of middle-class life. Life-styles had to express political commitment, while aesthetic taste was part of political consciousness. Thus the intellectual, the student, and the professor could take a crucial role in the vanguard of revolution—a role that the established socialist parties and trade unions had denied them. For earlier Jewish left-wing intellectuals, their particular socialism had provided hope for true emancipation, dissolving in the blinding light of a shared present and future an unusable past which had divided Jew from gentile.[43] The New Left was gentile for the most part, but for them the way out of their academic or bourgeois isolation was along much the same path that the earlier generation had traveled. They also wanted emancipation from a supposedly sterile society and a debased culture, as they saw it, attuned to the process of revolution. The Weimar left-wing heritage was especially appropriate for the revolt of those who had not come from the working class and whose setting was the university rather than the factory.

Apart from providing a revolutionary theory for a New Left, left-wing intellectuals in the Weimar Republic, whether under the influence of Hegel or Kant, began a new theoretical discourse which had lasting consequences for Marxist scholarship. Their greatest contribution may have been the application of new insights and different angles of vision to the past and their demonstration of how the past might become relevant to the present. Academic scholars such as Aby Warburg and Ernst Cassirer, Hegelian Marxists such as the young Georg Lukács, and Kantian Marxists such as many of those who wrote in *Die Weltbühne* began a process of intellectual questioning and debate that is still with us.

V

The End and a New Beginning?

THE GROWING ISOLATION of cultured and articulate German Jews had become a fact long before Adolf Hitler's declaration of war against the Jews in 1937: "I do not want to force the adversary into battle . . . instead, I tell him . . . I want to annihilate you! And then my cleverness will aid me in maneuvering you into a corner so that you cannot strike me, but I can pierce your heart."[1] The isolation of German Jews in Germany was due mainly but not solely to the waves of anti-Semitism which swept over the land. Much more dangerous anti-Semitic movements had existed in France before World War I, yet French Jewry was never so isolated. In Germany, however, with the lost war and the lost peace, the Jews' cultural emancipation turned back upon them. Its ideas had become deeply rooted among German Jews. Of course, they had also offered the best hope for Jewish assimilation, with their emphasis on the universality of reason and the possibility that anyone could attain citizenship through *Bildung*. Acceptance of these ideas was linked to the unique social structure of German Jewry; it was solidly middle class, with no poor and almost no peasants or workers. The transformation to the bourgeoisie of the Jews was perfect, and even young Jewish socialists who rejected bourgeois capitalism retained the core of this cultural emancipation.

Jews clung to an ideology that had been abandoned by most

Germans and upheld it under conditions which should have made its failure obvious; they flew its banner high under the Nazis, starting with the performance of *Nathan the Wise* as the inaugural play of the new ghetto theater. They lived the life of the cultured middle class even under the shadow of imminent death. It is no surprise, then, that the Jewish notables, cultured and respectable, failed to comprehend the Germans with whom they negotiated the fate of the Jews; apparently equally respectable and cultured, the Nazis whom they faced across the table liked to make a show of their *Bildung*. Although the Nazis prided themselves on a reinvigorated *Volk* community where everyone had an equal chance, in reality the traditional educational elite had increased its share of university students compared to the rest of the population.[2] But the *Bildung* of the National Socialists was no longer the *Bildung* of the German-Jewish tradition.

The patterns of thought we have analyzed led to dangerous illusions about the nature of the German people and the imperatives of modern politics. Jews were not the only group among Germans that failed to understand the need which chauvinist and racist nationalism filled in a time of crisis and the success of mass politics built upon such an irrational foundation—but for Jews this lack of understanding was fatal. Their belief in the primacy of culture subordinated politics to lofty principles. Adolf Hitler was underestimated as a former house painter, a member of the uncultured petty bourgeoisie. The famous Berlin theater critic Alfred Kerr even poured contempt on *Die Diktatur des Hausknechts* (*The Dictatorship of the Menial Servant* 1934), as he called it; Adolf Hitler was the embodiment of the mob—a mob which had read Nietzsche.[3] Yet in his book, contempt was paired with insight; for example, Kerr believed that as far as Germany was concerned, World War I had never ended; he felt that the Nazis were continuing the war through their lies, aggressiveness, and brutality. But it was in his title and his belittlement of the Nazis that Kerr expressed ideas current among many of his fellow German-Jewish exiles. German Jews had little experience in working with the extreme right; they believed that culture was a liberal and left monopoly. That culture could be successfully co-opted by the right seemed beyond reason, and they failed to see that the once noble elements of *Bildung* were, in fact, being used and distorted in the political liturgy of National Socialism. This liturgy made good use of the emphasis on aesthetics, classical motifs, and educational purpose. The link between *Bildung* and the Enlightenment had been destroyed; instead, *Bildung* was linked to racism and nationalism. National Socialism was merely the climax of a long development during which the *Bildung* of Humboldt, Lessing, and Goethe had become an ever narrower vision. The German Jews who have concerned us stood still while history advanced in an unforeseen direction.

In 1904, Rabbi Caesar Seligmann, a leader of the German-Jewish reform movement, preached a sermon in the great synagogue of Hamburg on the occasion of the centennial of Jewish orphanages founded on the educational principles of the eighteenth-century Enlightenment. His sermon summarized the history we have endeavored to isolate and examine. Before the emancipation of the Jews, he said, Judaism's will to live had died, and the Jews were surrounded by darkness. Suddenly, like a miracle, they were resurrected and light penetrated darkness. The theme of movement from darkness to light seems to accompany the history of German Jewry as a typical metaphor dating from the Enlightenment. How did this miracle occur? The fertilization of Judaism with German culture was the kiss that awakened the slumbering prince. Seligmann went on to exclaim, "Shall we tear a century of . . . German *Bildung* out of Jewish breasts?"[4] German Jews, he warned, must not be lulled to sleep by romantic notions of the past. They must remember what it was like to live as a Jew in Germany a century ago; they must acknowledge the tremendous tasks that were accomplished to raise German Jewry to a state of culture now taken for granted.[5]

Yet, Seligmann continued, we do not serve this culture well if we discard our Jewishness. The very survival of Judaism through the ages imposes a moral duty; it contains a categorical imperative which cannot be denied. The specifically Jewish does not oppose but complements German culture, for all men of goodwill share identical aspirations.[6] Here Seligmann turned to the concept of the Enlightenment to proclaim the identity of Judaism and German culture—all men shared an innate goodness and morality; they were part of the system of natural and moral laws decreed by God. This belief in God's natural and moral order, according to Seligmann, meant concern for the welfare of the state, which every religious community supported, as well as the cultivation of loyalty, reverence, and family feeling. The demands of the natural and moral order coincide with the needs of bourgeois society, as they did during the Enlightenment. Seligmann integrated Judaism into this natural and moral order; Jewish religious ceremonies symbolized man's moral obligations and his relationship to God. Here the Jewish and the German met in the deism of the Enlightenment, and this meeting was made possible through the power of German *Bildung,* which brings light into the Jewish soul.[7]

Seligmann was a leader of reform and liberal Judaism, but it must be clear from our discussion that the ideas which he put forward were to a greater or lesser extent those of most articulate and intellectual German Jews. They informed writers and scholars, liberals, and left-wing intellectuals. But they also played their role in German Zionism. In its attempt to construct a secular Jewish nation, the Jewish national awakening was influenced by German nationalism as well as by an appeal to specific Jewish biblical traditions. The German influence derived, for the most part, from that strand of German nationalism which had focused on solidarity rather than on domination and which had regarded the national community as encouraging, not aborting, individual self-fulfillment. This nationalism referred to Fichte and Herder as interpreted during the age of Jewish emancipation rather than taking its cue from the aggressive nationalism about to triumph over the older patriotic tradition in Germany. Hans Kohn, then a Zionist official, summarized in 1929 the ideals of a group of German Zionists, including Martin Buber and Robert Weltsch, the editor of the official German Zionist paper, the *Jüdische Rundschau.* Since 1909, when they had first met, he wrote, this group of friends had conceived Zionism as a movement through which they could realize their most fundamental personal convictions—pacifism, liberalism, and humanism.[8] Buber himself wrote a few years later that what was ethically wrong for the individual could not be regarded as right for the community, for the individual and the community were as one in the sight of God.[9] When the *Jüdische Rundschau* criticized the choice of *Nathan the Wise* as the first play performed by the *Kulturbund* in 1933, it specifically rejected any imputation of provincialism and instead demanded that Jews must be receptive to universal ideals—but as Jews.[10] Such sentiment appears vague, but, more specifically, loyalty to the *Volk* was regarded by these Zionists as a necessary step toward commitment to the needs of humanity. This was not a nationalism most Europeans would have recognized after World War I.

To be sure, the leader of German Zionism at the time, Kurt Blumenfeld, maintained that the nationally conscious Jew should maintain a certain distance between himself and German culture,[11] yet he himself appealed to the authorities of the German classical period. A clean separation may well have proved impossible, and it would be interesting to determine how much the elements of *Bildung* and the Enlightenment were incorporated into this self-conscious Jewish identity—into the Jewish history and tradition which they claimed as their own. This may be easier to learn from the writings of Martin Buber and his group, and even of Ahad Ha-am, the Hebraist of Odessa,[12] than from the younger men and women who advocated a more aggressive postassimilatory Zionism. After all, Martin Buber and his friends were united in the struggle for a Jewish-Arab binational state in Palestine.

These Zionists attempted to humanize nationalism in spite of the *Volkisch* vocabulary which sometimes crept into their language; as far as Buber was concerned, the soul of the individual had to embody the soul of the *Volk*. However, nationalism was not supposed to annihilate individual will and personality; on the contrary, for men such as Buber and Weltsch, affinity to the *Volk* meant cultivating one's own personality from out of one's Jewish substance. This self-cultivation differed from the concept of *Bildung* because of its emphasis on intuitive cognition and experience. Nevertheless, the goal was the same—a continuous process of individual self-expression. To be sure, all nationalism by its very nature stands close to the abyss of hatred toward other people and undue pride in one's own nation. But these Zionists tried to avoid such dangers through their ideal of community and their belief that the nation was merely a step toward a common humanity. Nathan the Wise entered once more, although through the back door, while the ideals of *Bildung* and Enlightenment were used to temper modern nationalism. It was not merely because of the weakness of the Jewish people—without an army and without a state—that such men advocated their humanist, even pacifist, nationalism but rather from a deep conviction that the Jewish nation must differ from others in its love for all mankind and respect for the dignity and potential of the individual.

The attempt to humanize nationalism is one of the most important legacies of German Jewry, although Zionists from eastern Europe shared these ideals. Aron David Gordon, for example, who had emigrated from Russia to Palestine in 1904, inspired Zionists such as Hans Kohn and Hugo Bergmann, men of German culture, who used his term "the human people" as the title of one of their books. Gordon's belief that a people cannot be redeemed by political success and even less through military victory, but only through their moral and spiritual rebirth, spoke to the ideals of the German Zionists.[13] This is a part of Zionist history which demands to be written, and although it was to be aborted when it clashed with political reality, it did represent one of the few attempts in recent times to steer a national revival from a narrow and provincial vision to a larger humanist ideal, calling on patriotism rather than a nationalism which had plunged Europe into some of the bloodiest wars of its history.

Jewish orthodoxy, like Zionism, was influenced by the cultural emancipation of German Jews. Samson Raphael Hirsch, its leader, thought that freedom under the law, virtue, and morality, as proclaimed by the age of Jewish emancipation, were based upon Jewish thought and Jewish values "which sang their way into the hearts of the German people." Still, he continued, it was a noble spirit like Schiller who had made it possible for Jews to live like human beings among humanity.[14] German-Jewish orthodoxy did not want to return to the ghetto and accepted emancipation as joyfully as Caesar Seligmann, the leader of Jewish reform. The return to a past remembered as depriving Jews of their very humanity was not a viable alternative for any segment of German Jewry.

We have shown that what once had been a part of German culture became a central Jewish heritage. To understand this redefinition of the Jewish substance, we must look at the history of German Jewry from the perspective of its emancipation rather than from our knowledge of its brutal extermination, which hardly any Jews or gentiles could have envisioned during most of its history.

Obviously, not all German Jews shared these ideals; among more than half a million men and women, there were many varieties of thought and opinion, especially since most German Jews were educated and articulate. Even so, the heritage of the cultural emancipation found a continuing place in their daily lives.

Moreover, to whatever extent the German heritage of *Bildung* and the Enlightenment had informed the Jewish substance of men and women, this heritage was used to fight a new ghettoization once the Nazis excluded Jews from German cultural life. Just as newly emancipated Jews had appropriated this German culture as their own, so the Jews about to become disenfranchised turned to *Bildung* and the Enlightenment in order to keep the door open to the gentile world, to create a space where they could remain German Jews. When the *Kulturbund Deutscher Juden* was founded in 1933, Julius Bab explicitly denied that the Jews wanted to erect their own ghetto walls through this cultural organization: "We do not want to cultivate a one-dimensional Jewish culture but the grand German culture whose soil nourished us," for this culture, he continued, "represents the most dignified approach to all that is human, an integral part of Jewishness."[15] It would be difficult to find a better summary of what German culture meant to German Jews—how it had become part of their very substance.

This reaffirmation of German culture was made at a time when the Jewish cultural ghetto was not yet a total reality, for until the tightening of anti-Jewish polices in November 1938, Jews could attend German cultural events and were not dependent upon the *Kulturbund* for such sustenance. After November 1938, they had to turn to the *Kulturbund;* however, it now led a shadow existence, its activities directed toward encouraging Jewish emigration from Germany.[16] Thus even though the *Kulturbund* had to compete with the German cultural scene for its audiences during the first five years of the Third Reich, it forced upon German Jewry a discussion of what had been "Jewish" in their cultural emancipation.

Hans Hinkel, the Nazi official charged with control over Jewish cultural life, told a Nazi party newspaper that the *Kulturbund* could present pieces written either by Jews or by non-Jews who dealt with Jewish themes, while names like Shakespeare, Molière, Verdi, Johann Strauss, Shaw, and Ibsen occupied a prominent place in the repertory. Requests to perform works by Beethoven, Mozart, and Goethe bordered on presumption and had to be rejected. Foreign literature was allowed, but German cultural goods had to be protected. Yet Mozart's *Magic Flute*, Beethoven, and Schubert were all part of the 1936 program of the *Kulturbund*.[17] The inconsistencies of Hinkel's censorship can perhaps be explained by the pressure he faced from local party organizations. For example, a Berlin branch of the Nazi Party complained to its propaganda officer about the tactlessness of performing *Fidelio* with an all-Jewish cast in Nazi Germany and was angry when the *Kulturbund Newsletter* praised Goethe: "What do Goethe and Beethoven have in common with the Jews?"[18] The answer should have been, "Much more than present-day Germans," but Hinkel, who had joined the Nazi Party in 1921 (his membership number was 287), was hardly the person to perceive this truth; for all his boasting that the *Kulturbund* proved the Nazis' generosity toward their greatest enemy, he spent much of his career as a journalist attacking the Jews as "masters of lies."[19]

The *Kulturbund* took full advantage of the non-German classics. In addition, since Austria was treated as a foreign country until 1938, so-called German works did slip by in the early days. German Jews could now claim *Nathan the Wise* as truly their own, for Lessing's play was no longer permitted on the German stage.[20]

The *Kulturbund* made the most of the "grand culture" it could present while agonizing about the new definition of Jewishness demanded by the times. No clear definition was in sight: at the plenary meeting of the *Kulturbund* in 1936, the group explicitly rejected once again the formation of any "cultural ghetto" and proclaimed that no uniquely Jewish culture existed but that the great classical works which belonged to all mankind could be presented in a Jewish framework.[21] Georg Hermann, the author of *Jettchen Gebert*, praised by a lecturer of the *Kulturbund* as exemplifying the best traditions of the German-Jewish past,[21] responded in 1936 to an inquiry about the future of Jewish literature. He asserted that so-called Jewish literature was merely literature written and felt by Jews, while Hebrew and Yiddish literature had, at best, a future only in Palestine.[23] When writing about the *Kulturbund* theater, one Jewish newspaper tried to cut the gordian knot

by asserting that content did not determine cultural values but that
the actor himself must portray Jewish dignity and character to the
audience through his comportment, whatever the play.[24]

German Jews had been robbed of their German-Jewish identity and did not know where to turn; it had been far easier to find a
new identity in the heady days of emancipation than when confronted with a sudden ghettoization. To cling to the by now traditional values was an understandable reaction, just as the former
leaders of the Jewish women's organization (*Jüdischer Frauenbund*) were found reading Goethe as they waited for deportation.[25]
Eastern European Jewish culture was not accepted as a valid substitute; indeed, the *Kulturbund* believed that outside the religious
sphere it was fragmentary at best and did not represent a cultural
unity.[26] Who would want to return to a ghetto past, remembering
how Jews had lived without dignity, as tradition had it, their very
humanity stripped away? Indeed, when the first German-Jewish
painter, Moritz Oppenheim, painted scenes from the ghetto
shortly after emancipation, it was transformed, as we have seen,
into a community permeated with German middle-class values[27]—
lifted from darkness into light. Against such a background, it is not
difficult to account for the lack of interest by *Kulturbund* audiences in plays translated from the Yiddish or the Hebrew.[28] Instead, the new Jewish ghetto resisted being pushed back into darkness through a new, and for them archaic, definition of Jewishness
and continued to seek solace in *Bildung* and the Enlightenment.

The inconsistency of Hinkel's censorship, noted already, permitted Jews to comment publicly in 1936 on the hundredth anniversary of Wilhelm von Humboldt's death. Once more, they
could look to true *Bildung* in dark times. *Der Morgen,* a Jewish
journal which had always been committed to the ideals of *Bildung*
and the Enlightenment, recalled that at the 1867 celebration of
Humboldt's hundredth birthday, a Jew, the philosopher Heymann
Steinthal, had addressed the German students. Times had changed
but not the commitment of German Jews to these ideals, as the
journal confirmed when it continued, "We are no longer allowed
to raise our voices at the hundredth anniversary of Humboldt's
death. However, with gratitude, we wish to pledge our allegiance
to Humboldt's ideals, for together with Lessing and Kant, Goethe
and Schiller, they represent that inner German spirit of which we

are a part and which we can never lose as long as it informs our striving."[29]

Yet by 1940 it seemed that Nazi pressure had succeeded in bringing about the final cultural separation between German and Jew. The catalog of books sold by the *Kulturbund,* no longer printed but mimeographed, contained no German works, not even milestones of the German-Jewish symbiosis like Georg Hermann's *Jettchen Gebert.* Eastern European Jewish literature dominated the list, together with works by German Jews about eastern European ghettos and works by writers considered by the Nazis to be typically Jewish, such as Heinrich Heine and Moses Mendelssohn.[30] Yet a listed biography of Moses Mendelssohn for Jewish youth, written before the Nazi seizure of power, advocates the ideals of tolerance, friendship between Christians and Jews, and the acceptance of the German language and customs.[31] This was probably not the only work which claimed to deal with a uniquely Jewish subject but in reality continued to praise the best of German culture.

The history of German Jewry was drawing to a close and with it that definition of Jewishness we have endeavored to trace. Yet when Nathan remained behind on the stage, lonely and forlorn, as the sultan and the templar marched out arm in arm, appearances proved deceptive. Behind Nathan stood new generations eager to take up a heritage thought long dead and forgotten. We have sketched only a part of this heritage—mainly as it affected the academic disciplines and left-wing intellectuals—yet the ideal of *Bildung* based on the Enlightenment continued to find new adherents in Germany after World War II. To be sure, this heritage is difficult to trace; direct and unambiguous references to the German-Jewish tradition are few. But as this tradition is disentangled from the general history of German Jews as a specific form of Jewish identity, we will find measuring its legacy an easier task.

That this heritage contained much of what was best and most noble in German culture seems obvious. Self-cultivation, tolerance, and rationality are still very promising ideals in a volatile world, while the humanizing of society, of Marxism, and, above all, of nationalism is a pressing concern for survival. German Jews after emancipation took on a Jewish substance which commanded respect; they acted from a perceived necessity as they were pushed by the process of emancipation into assuming a new Jewish identity. This Jewish identity did not, for the most part, exclude the maintenance of religious beliefs, ritual, and ceremonies. We have mentioned these only occasionally, because we are concerned here with a secular identity in an increasingly secular age.

The German-Jewish dialogue did take place, and in it the Jews came to exemplify a German humanist tradition which at one time had provided the space for Germans and Jews to meet in friendship. The humanist ideals of *Bildung* and the Enlightenment lived on, even under the Nazis. Among liberals and left-wing intellectuals, the flame was kept alive from exile; whether it continued to burn inside Germany is more difficult to determine. But it was the German-Jewish *Bildungsbürgertum* which, more than any other single group, preserved Germany's better self across dictatorship, war, holocaust, and defeat.

NOTES

1. A Cultural Emancipation

1. Jacob Toury, *Soziale und Politische Geschichte der Juden in Deutschland* (Düsseldorf, 1977), p. 112.

2. Quoted in Eva G. Reichmann, *Grösse und Verhängnis deutsch-jüdischer Existenz* (Heidelberg, 1974), p. 22.

3. David Frankel, ed., *Sulamith, Eine Zeitschrift zur Beförderung der Kultur und Humanität unter den Israeliten,* Jahrg. 3, 2(1811):239.

4. This definition derives from David Sorkin, "Wilhelm von Humboldt: The Theory and Practice of Self-Formation *(Bildung)*, 1791–1810," *Journal of the History of Ideas* (January 1983):55–73. This is one of the best discussions of the meaning of *Bildung; see also* David Sorkin, "Ideology and Identity: Political Emancipation and the Emergence of a Jewish Subculture in Germany, 1800–1948" (Ph.D. diss., University of California, Berkeley, 1983). I am much indebted to this work.

5. Hans Weil, *Die Entstehung des Deutschen Bildungsprinzips* (Bonn, 1930), p. 47.

6. Johann Wolfgang von Goethe, *Wilhelm Meister's Apprenticeship* (New York, 1962), p. 274.

7. Sorkin, "Ideology and Identity," p. 20.

8. Hans Bayer, "Zur Soziologie des Bürgerlichen Bildungsbegriffs," *Paedagogica Historica* 15(1975):331, n. 1.

9. Berthold Auerbach, *Schrift und Volk* (Leipzig, 1846), p. 323.

10. *Ibid.,* p. 300.

11. Ignaz Maybaum, *Synagogue and Society: Jewish-Christian Collaboration in the Defense of Western Civilization* (London, 1944), p. 86.

12. Toury, *Soziale und Politische Geschichte,* p. 112; Heinz Holeczek, "The Jews and the German Liberals," *Yearbook XXVIII* (Leo Baeck Institute, 1983), p. 80.

13. Auerbach, *Schrift und Volk,* pp. 267–68.

14. Berthold Auerbach, *Neue Dorfgeschichten,* vol. 1 (Stuttgart, 1876), p. 86.

15. Klemens Felden, "Die Übernahme des antisemitischen Stereotyps als soziale Norm durch die bürgerliche Gesellschaft Deutschlands, 1875–1900" (Ph.D. diss., Heidelberg, 1962), p. 33.

16. Brief, 9 April 1881, *Berthold Auerbach Briefe and seinen Freund Jakob Auerbach,* vol. 2 (Frankfurt am Main, 1884), p. 453.

17. George L. Mosse, *The Crisis of German Ideology* (New York, 1965), pp. 25, 26.

18. Weil, *Die Entstehung,* p. 149.

83

19. *Sulamith,* Jahr. 3, 2(1808):182.
20. Friedrich Schiller, *Über die ästhetische Erziehung des Menschen* (Stuttgart, 1965), p. 36.
21. Thomas Nipperdey, *Deutsche Geschichte 1800–1866* (Munich, 1983), p. 540.
22. Wilhelm von Humboldt, "Wesen der Schönheit," *Gesammelte Werke* (Berlin, 1843):344.
23. *Sulamith,* Jahrg. 1 (1806):9.
24. G. Salomon, *Auswahl mehrerer Predigten zunächst für Israeliten* (Dessau, 1818), *passim; Israelitisches Predigt- und Schul-Magazin* 1(Magdeburg, 1834):8.
25. Wilhelm von Humboldt, "Ideen zu einem Versuch, die Grenzen der Wirksamkeit des Staates zu bestimmen," *Werke in Fünf Bänden,* vol. 1 (Stuttgart, 1960), p. 105.
26. Benno Offenburg, "Das Erwachen des deutschen Nationalbewustseins in der Preussischen Judenheit" (Ph.D. diss., University of Hamburg, 1933), p. 61; Karl Schwarz, *Die Juden in der Kunst* (Berlin, 1928), p. 123.
27. *Zuruf an die Jünglinge welche den Fahnen des Vaterlands folgen* (Berlin, 1813), p. 58.
28. Christoph Prignitz, *Vaterlandsliebe und Freiheit. Deutscher Patriotismus 1750 bis 1850* (Wiesbaden, 1981), p. 31.
29. Karl Hoffmann, *Des Teutschen Volkes Feuriger Dank und Ehrentempel* (Offenbach, 1815), pp. 259, 536.
30. Rudolf Vierhaus, " 'Patriotismus'—Begriff und Realität einer moralisch-politischen Haltung," *Deutsche patriotische und gemeinnützige Gesellschaften, Wolfenbüttler Forschungen* 8(n.d.):15.
31. Prignitz, *Vaterlandsliebe und Freiheit,* p. 133.
32. *Ibid.,* p. 134.
33. Sorkin, "Wilhelm von Humboldt," p. 60.
34. *Ibid.,* p. 72.
35. Auerbach, *Schrift und Volk,* p. 322.
36. Goethe, *Wilhelm Meister's Apprenticeship,* p. 206.
37. Gotthold Ephraim Lessing, *Die Juden* (scene 21), quoted in Paul R. Mendes-Flohr and Jehuda Reinharz, eds., *The Jews in the Modern World* (New York and Oxford, 1981), p. 56.
38. Moses Mendelssohn, *Ungedrucktes und Unbekanntes von ihm und über ihn,* ed. M. Kayserling (Leipzig, 1883), p. 21.
39. Berthold Auerbach, *Dichter und Kaufmann, ein Lebensgemälde aus der Zeit Moses Mendelssohns,* vol. 1; *Berthold Auerbachs gesammelte Schriften,* vol. 12 (Stuttgart, 1864), p. 208.
40. Ludwig Geiger, *Geschichte der Juden in Berlin* (Berlin, 1871), p. 107.
41. J. Wolf, *Sechs Deutsche Reden gehalten in der Synagoge zu Dessau, etc.,* vol. 2 (Dessau, 1813), p. 16.
42. George L. Mosse, *Nationalism and Sexuality, Respectability and Abnormal Sexuality in Modern Europe* (New York, 1985), ch. IV.
43. Nipperdey, *Deutsche Geschichte,* p. 540.
44. Theodor Fontane, *Jenny Treibel* (New York, 1976), p. 80.
45. F. Paulsen, *Das deutsche Bildungswesen in seiner geschichtlichen Entwicklung* (Leipzig and Berlin, 1906), pp. 110–14.
46. Ernst Bloch, *Das Prinzip der Hoffnung,* 2 vols. (Frankfurt am Main, 1959), especially vol. 1.

47. Kenneth Barkin, "Social Control and the Volksschule in Vormärz Prussia," *Central European History* 16 (March 1983): 32; Peter Berglar, *Wilhelm von Humboldt* (Reinbeck bei Hamburg, 1970), p. 87.

48. Rüdiger vom Bruch, *Wissenschaft, Politik und öffentliche Meinung, Gelehrtenpolitik im Wilhelminischen Deutschland (1890–1914)* (Husum, 1980), especially pp. 414–26.

49. *Das Tagebuch* (26 September 1933): 1526.

50. Christian Boeck, *Schleiermachers Vaterländisches Wirken 1806–1813* (Berlin, 1920), pp. 7, 10; Leonard Krieger, *The German Idea of Freedom* (Boston, 1957), pp. 183 ff.

51. Fritz K. Ringer, *The Decline of the German Mandarins: The German Academic Community, 1890–1933* (Cambridge, 1969), p. 136.

52. George L. Mosse, "Friendship and Nationhood: About the Promise and Fulfillment of German Nationalism," *Journal of Contemporary History* 17 (April 1982): 358.

53. George L. Mosse, *Towards the Final Solution* (New York, 1978), ch. 2.

54. Walter Benjamin to Ludwig Strauss, 7 January 1913. Jewish National and University Library, Jerusalem, Archives Ms. Var. 424, 196/9, p. 4.

55. "Gespräch mit Maria Jahoda," *Ästhetik und Kommunikation*, no. 51 (June 1983): 72.

56. Jehuda Reinharz, ed., *Dokumente zur Geschichte des Deutschen Zionismus, 1882–1933* (Tübingen, 1981), p. 138.

57. Ernest Bloch, *Auswahl aus seinen Schriften*, ed. Hans Heinz Holz (Frankfurt am Main, 1967), p. 158.

58. *Caesar Seligmann (1860–1950). Erinnerungen* (Frankfurt am Main, 1975), p. 143.

59. Hannah Arendt, quoted in Karl S. Guthke, "Lessing und das Judentum. Rezeption. Dramatik und Kritik. Krypto-Spinozismus," *Wolfenbüttler Studien zur Aufklärung* 4 (Wolfenbüttel, 1977): 236.

60. Gabriel Riesser, *Einige Worte über Lessing's Denkmal* (Frankfurt am Main, 1881, first published 1831), p. 7.

61. *Allgemeine Zeitung des Judentums*, Jahrg. 45, no. 7 (15 February 1881): 100.

62. Riesser, *Einige Worte*, pp. 12, 13.

63. Elizabeth Petuchowski, "Zur Lessing-Rezeption in der deutsch-jüdischen Presse. Lessing's 200. Geburtstag (22. Januar 1929)," *Lessing Yearbook XIV* (1980), p. 47.

64. *Ibid.*

65. Julius Bab, "Kulturbund Deutscher Juden," *Der Schild*, Jahrg. 12, no. 17 (14 September 1933): 148: *Jüdische Rundschau*, no. 79/80 (4. IX. 1933), p. 624.

66. Herbert Freeden, *Jüdisches Theater in Deutschland* (Tübingen, 1964), p. 27.

67. *Jüdische Rundschau*, no. 59, (25. VIII. 1933), p. 363; *Ibid.*, no. 63 (8. VIII. 1933), p. 405.

68. Modris Eksteins, *The Limits of Reason: The German Democratic Press and the Collapse of the Weimar Republic* (Oxford, 1975), pp. 37, 118. For the influential German-Jewish philosopher Hermann Cohen, the release of Captain Dreyfus from prison was a messianic event. Nathan Rotenstreich, "Hermann Cohen's Position in the Development of Nineteenth and Twentieth Century Philosophy and His Philosophy of Judaism," *International Conference on German Jews* (Clark University, Worcester, Mass., October 8–11, 1983).

69. Eksteins, *The Limits of Reason*, p. 307.
70. George L. Mosse, *Masses and Man* (New York, 1980), p. 155.
71. *Sulamith*, Jahrg. 1 (Leipzig, 1806): 128.
72. Marjorie Lamberti, *Jewish Activism in Imperial Germany* (New Haven and London, 1978), pp. 25, 37, and *passim*.
73. Rabbiner Dr. Werner, *Judentaufen* (Rede zum C. V. 9 February 1910), *Im Deutschen Reich*, Feldbücherei des C. V. (n.d.), pp. 22, 42.
74. Stefan Zweig, *Die Welt von Gestern* (Frankfurt am Main, 1962), p. 105.
75. Leon Botstein, "Stefan Zweig and the Illusion of the Jewish European," in Marion Sonnenfeld, ed., *Stefan Zweig* (Albany, New York, 1983), especially pp. 90, 92.
76. David Turner, "The Humane Ideal in Stefan Zweig's *Novelle:* Some Complications and Limitations," in Sonnenfeld, ed., *Stefan Zweig*, p. 160.

2. German Jews and German Popular Culture

1. George L. Mosse, *The Crisis of German Ideology* (New York, 1964), pp. 243–44; Rudolf Kaula, *Der Liberalismus und die Deutschen Juden. Das Judentum als konservatives Element* (Munchen and Leipzig, 1918), p. 99. For the conflict between traditionalists and modernists in the Weimar Republic, see Walter Laqueur, *Weimar Culture* (New York, 1974), ch. 4 and ch. 5.
2. Gustav Wyneken, *Wickersdorf* (Lauenburg, Elbe, 1922), p. 33.
3. While some Jews continued to support Bayreuth, some, such as Rudolf Pringsheim, left after Wagner's increasingly violent anti-Semitic outbursts. Cosima Wagner, *Die Tagebücher*, vol. 2 (1878–84) (Munich and Zürich, 1977), p. 162.
4. Leo Baeck, *Das Wesen des Judentums* (Frankfurt am Main, 1926), p. 281.
5. Paul R. Mendes-Flohr, "The Study of the Jewish Intellectual: Some Methodological Proposals," in F. Malino and P. Cohen Albert, eds., *Essays in Modern Jewish History: A Tribute to Ben Halpern* (Rutherford, N.J.: Fairleigh Dickinson, 1981), p. 161.
6. David Turner, "The Humane Ideal in Stefan Zweig's *Novelle:* Some Complications and Limitations," in Marion Sonnenfeld, ed., *Stefan Zweig* (Albany, New York, 1983), p. 158.
7. Emil Ludwig, *Genie und Charakter, Zwanzig Männliche Bildnisse* (Berlin, 1925), pp. 275, 281. These comments were made in a hostile portrait of the melancholy and homosexual writer Hermann Bang.
8. Berthold Auerbach, *Schrift und Volk* (Leipzig, 1946), pp. 58, 80, 92.
9. Leo Löwenthal, *Literatur und Gesellschaft* (Neuwied and Berlin, 1964), p. 196, n. 3.
10. Emil Ludwig, *Geschenke des Lebens. Ein Rückblick* (Berlin, 1931), pp. 103–104.
11. *Ibid.*, p. 573.
12. D. A. Prater, *European of Yesterday: A Biography of Stefan Zweig* (Oxford, 1972), p. 316.
13. Martin Buber, *Briefwechsel aus sieben Jahrzehnten*, ed. Grete Schaeder, vol. 1 (1897–1918) (Heidelberg, 1972), p. 431.
14. *Ibid.*, p. 499.
15. Quoted in Erich Fitzbauer, ed., *Stefan Zweig, durch Zeiten und Welten* (Graz and Vienna, 1961), p. 27.
16. Emil Ludwig, *Wilhelm der Zweite* (Berlin, 1928), p. 10.

17. Annamaria Rucktaschel and Hans Dieter Zimmermann, eds., *Trivial-literatur* (Munich, 1976), p. 233.

18. Emil Ludwig, *Kunst und Schicksal, vier Bildnisse* (Bern, 1953, first published 1927), p. 7.

19. Leon Edel, *Bloomsbury* (New York, 1961), p. 253.

20. Stefan Zweig, *Sternstunden der Menschheit* (Insel Bucherei, n.d.), p. 116.

21. Biographies in Ludwig, *Genie und Charakter, passim.*

22. "Walther Rathenaus Weltbild," *Gemeindeblatt der Jüdischen Gemeinde zu Berlin,* Jahrg. 17, no. 7 (1 July 1927): 1.

23. Stefan Zweig, "Walther Rathenau," in *Europäisches Erbe* (Frankfurt am Main, 1960), p. 922.

24. Ludwig, *Genie und Charakter,* p. 141.

25. Zweig, *Europäisches Erbe,* p. 238.

26. Walther Rathenau, *Zur Kritik der Zeit* (Berlin, 1912), p. 219.

27. For example, although critical of Rathenau's talent for friendship, see Count Harry Kessler, *Walther Rathenau: His Life and Work* (New York, 1969), ch. V.

28. Leonard Baker, *Days of Sorrow and Pain: Leo Baeck and the Berlin Jews* (New York and Toronto, 1978), p. 99.

29. Ludwig, *Genie und Charakter,* pp. 51, 54.

30. *Ibid.,* p. 256.

31. Prater, *European of Yesterday,* p. 399.

32. Emil Ludwig, *Führer Europas nach der Natur gezeichnet* (Amsterdam, 1934), pp. 10–11.

33. Alfred Wolf, "Stefan Zweig and Judaism—A Letter and an Interview," *Judaism* 31 (Spring 1952): 242.

34. *Der Jude, Sonderheft Antisemitismus und Jüdisches Volkstum* (1925), p. 132.

35. Prater, *European of Yesterday,* p. 270.

36. This is suggested by Helmut Gruber, *The Politics of German Literature, 1914 to 1933: A Study of the Expressionists and Objectivists* (Ann Arbor, Mich.: University Microfilms, 1962), p. 196.

37. Emil Ludwig, *Der Menschensohn* (Berlin, 1928), p. 262.

38. Ludwig Marcuse noted this point in "Die Emil Ludwig Front," *Das Tagebuch,* p. 12(1931):142.

39. Emil Ludwig, *An die Laterne! Bilder aus der Revolution* (Charlottenburg, 1919), pp. 55, 83.

40. Stefan Zweig, *Die Welt von Gestern.* (Berlin, 1962), p. 219; Martin Buber, *Briefwechsel aus sieben Jahrzehnten,* vol. 2 (1918–38) (Heidelberg, 1973), p. 17.

41. For a good expression of his ideas on this subject, see Stefan Zweig, *Erasmus of Rotterdam* (New York, 1934), pp. 3–13.

42. Stefan Zweig, *Briefe an Freunde,* ed. Richard Friedenthal (Frankfurt Am Main, 1978), p. 153.

43. Prater, *European of Yesterday,* p. 174.

44. Zweig's contrast between humanism and politics is clearly stated in Zweig, *Erasmus of Rotterdam,* pp. 243–44.

45. *Ibid.,* p. 228.

46. George L. Mosse, "What Germans Really Read," *Masses and Man* (New York, 1980), pp. 52–69.

47. *Die Gartenlaube*, no. 20 (1882):451–55; *Die Gartenlaube*, no. 19 (1881): 308–14.

48. Mosse, "Death, Time, and History: *Volk*ish Utopia and its Transcendence," *Masses and Man*, pp. 69–86.

49. *Ibid.*, pp. 69–71. I am discussing the apocalyptic and millenarian tradition as it affected the political right—a counterweight to the liberal tradition of German Jewry. But this German revolution took many forms; it was also part of the so-called life reform movement and influenced the many wandering semi-anarchist prophets in Weimar Germany. Ulrich Linse, *Barfüssige Propheten. Erlöser der zwanziger Jahre* (Berlin, 1983), *passim*.

50. Heinrich Anacker, *Die Fanfare, Gedichte der Erhebung* (Munich, 1936), p. 116.

51. David Gross, "Marxism and Utopia: Ernst Bloch," *Towards A New Marxism* (St. Louis, 1973), pp. 85–100.

52. Steven E. Aschheim, *Brothers and Strangers: The East European Jew in German and German Jewish Consciousness, 1800–1923* (Madison, Wisc., 1982), ch. 6; Some who were inspired by Buber's tales to become active Jews and Zionists remained so, for example, Salman Schocken, founder of the Schocken publishing house and of the Hebrew daily, *Haaretz*. Stephen M. Poppel, "Salman Schocken and the Schocken Verlag," *Yearbook XVII* (Leo Baeck Institute, 1974), p. 93, n. 2.

53. Martin Buber, "Bildung und Weltanschauung" (Frankfurter Lehrhausrede), *Mittelstelle für Jüdische Erwachsenen Bildung, Reichsvertretung der Juden in Deutschland* (Frankfurt, April 1937), p. 1.

54. George L. Mosse, *Germans and Jews* (New York, 1970), pp. 85–89.

55. *Ibid.*, pp. 90–92.

56. Jakob Wassermann, "Fragment über das Nationalgefühl," *Lebensdienst* (Leipzig and Zürich, 1928), p. 190.

57. Jakob Wassermann, *Mein Weg als Deutscher und Jude* (Berlin, 1921), pp. 76 ff.

58. Jakob Wassermann, *Caspar Hauser* (Berlin, 1908), pp. 45, 62–63.

59. Siegmund Bing, *Jakob Wassermann* (Berlin, 1933), p. 82.

60. Wassermann, *Mein Weg als Deutscher und Jude*, p. 103.

61. *Ibid.*, p. 91.

62. Although Zweig praised Ludwig's biography of Goethe, he also seems to have considered Ludwig shallow and too much of an aesthete on occasion. Johanna Roden, "Stefan Zweig and Emil Ludwig," in *Stefan Zweig*, Sonnenfeld, ed., pp. 236–45.

63. Jakob Wassermann, "Rede über die Humanität" (1922), *Bekenntnisse und Begegnungen* (Bamberg, 1950), p. 127.

64. Wassermann, "Fragment über das Nationalgefühl," pp. 120, 190.

65. Marta Karlweiss, *Jakob Wassermann* (Berlin, 1933), p. 336.

66. Wassermann, *Mein Weg als Deutscher und Jude*, p. 116.

3. Intellectual Authority And Scholarship

1. Herbert Freeden, *Jüdisches Theater in Nazideutschland* (Tübingen, 1964), pp. 94–95.

2. Friedrich Andrae, ed., *Volksbücherei und Nationalsozialismus* (Wiesbaden, 1970), p. 147.

3. George L. Mosse, *Toward the Final Solution: A History of European Racism* (New York, 1978), ch. 10.

4. Christoph Prignitz, *Vaterlandsliebe und Freiheit* (Wiesbaden, 1981), p. 116.

5. Hans Kohn, *Martin Buber, Sein Werk und seine Zeit* (Köln, 1961), p. 95.

6. Sidney M. Bolkosky, *The Distorted Image: German-Jewish Perceptions of Germans and Germany, 1918–1935* (New York, 1975), p. 139.

7. *Ibid.*, p. 93; Samuel Meisels, *Goethe im Ghetto. Kleine Beiträge zu einem grossen Thema* (Wien, 1932), p. 29.

8. Albert Bielschowsky, *Goethe, Sein Leben und Seine Werke*, vol. 1 (Munich, 1914), pp. i, ix.

9. *Ibid.*, pp. 2, 369.

10. *Ibid.*, pp. x, 1.

11. Wolfgang Goetz, *Fünfzig Jahre Goethe-Gesellschaft* (Weimar, 1936), p. 13; *Mitglieder Verzeichnis der Goethe-Gesellschaft* (Weimar, 1926), *passim.* The predominance of Jews in Goethe research was one fact upon which Jews and Nazis could agree, though with quite different conclusions. Meisels, *Goethe im Ghetto*, pp. 10–12; Franz Koch, "Goethe und die Juden," *Erforschungen zur Judenfrage*, vol. 2 (Hamburg, 1937), p. 118.

12. Albert Ludwig, *Schiller und die deutsche Nachwelt* (Berlin, 1909), p. 109.

13. Karl Robert Mandelkow, ed., *Goethe im Urteil seiner Kritiker*, vol. 1 (Munich, 1977), p. 72.

14. *Ibid.*, pp. 316–21.

15. Wolfgang Lepmann, *Goethe und die Deutschen* (Stuttgart, 1962), p. 246.

16. Nehemia Anton Nobel, "Goethe, sein Verhältnis zu Religion und Religionen," *Bulletin des Leo Baeck Instituts*, Jahrg. 12, no. 48 (1969):323, 326.

17. Berthold Auerbach, *Epilog zur Lessing-Feier* (Dresden, 1850), pp. 8–9.

18. J. Riesser, "Widmung an Berthold Auerbach" in Gabriel Riesser, *Einige Worte über Lessing's Denkmal* (Frankfurt am Main, 1881). This is a reprint of the original 1831 call for a Lessing monument.

19. George L. Mosse, *The Nationalization of the Masses* (New York, 1975), ch. 3.

20. George L. Mosse, *The Crisis of German Ideology* (New York, 1964), pp. 64–65; see also Theodore Ziolkowski, "Der Hunger nach dem Mythos," in Reinhold Grimm and Jost Hermand, eds., in *Die sogenannten Zwanziger Jahre* (Bad Homburg, 1970), pp. 169-201.

21. Philip Rieff, *Freud: The Mind of the Moralist* (New York, 1961), p. 263.

22. Sigmund Freud, *The Interpretation of Dreams* (New York, 1965), p. 617.

23. Carl E. Schorske, *Fin-de-Siècle Vienna: Politics and Culture* (New York, 1980), pp. 187-88.

24. Dennis B. Klein, *The Jewish Origins of the Psychoanalytic Movement* (New York, 1981), pp. 150–51.

25. Rieff, *Freud*, p. 253.

26. Klein, *The Jewish Origins*, p. 141.

27. *Briefwechsel von Sigmund Freud und Arnold Zweig*, ed. Ernst L. Freud (Frankfurt am Main, 1968), p. 37.

28. David James Fisher, "Sigmund Freud and Romain Rolland: The Terrestrial Animal and His Great Oceanic Friend," *American Imago*, 33 (Spring 1976):1–59.

29. Emil Ludwig, *Der Entzauberte Freud* (Zurich, 1946), pp. 18, 21.

30. George L. Mosse, *Nationalism and Sexuality, Respectability and Abnormal Sexuality in Modern Europe* (New York, 1985), pp. 39–40.

31. Felix Gilbert, "From Art History to the History of Civilization: Gombrich's Biography of Aby Warburg," *Journal of Modern History,* 44 (September 1971): 385.

32. Gertrud Bing, "A. M. Warburg" (1965), in Aby M. Warburg, *Ausgewählte Schriften und Würdigungen,* ed. Dieter Wuttke (Baden-Baden, 1979), p. 461.

33. E. H. Gombrich, *Aby Warburg: An Intellectual Biography* (London, 1970), p. 308; Werner Kaegi, "Das Werk Aby Warburgs," *Neue Schweizer Rundschau,* Jahrg. 1 (1933):187.

34. Kaegi, "Das Werk Aby Warburgs," p. 288.

35. Gombrich, *Aby Warburg,* p. 21.

36. Bing, "A. M. Warburg," p. 452.

37. Gertrud Bing, *Aby M. Warburg* (Hamburg, 1958), p. 29; Peter Gay, "Weimar Culture," in Donald Fleming and Bernard Baylin, eds., *The Intellectual Migration* (Cambridge, Mass., 1969), p. 39.

38. Hans Liebeschütz, "Aby Warburg (1866–1929) as Interpreter of Civilization," *Yearbook XVI* (Leo Baeck Institute, 1971), pp. 229–30.

39. Gombrich, *Aby Warburg,* p. 228.

40. *Ibid.,* pp. 13–14.

41. Erwin Panofsky, *Meaning in the Visual Arts* (New York, 1955), pp. 15–16, 19.

42. Erwin Panofsky, *Studies in Iconology: Humanistic Themes in the Art of the Renaissance* (New York, 1962, first published 1939), pp. 229–30.

43. David R. Lipton, *Ernst Cassirer: The Dilemma of a Liberal Intellectual in Germany, 1914–33* (Toronto, 1978), pp. 92–93, 131.

44. Ernst Cassirer, *Critical Idealism as Philosophy of Culture,* cited in Maurizio Serra, "Sui miti e la crisi storica dell umanesimo borghese negli anni trenta," *Storia Contemporanea* 14 (October 1983):585.

45. Ernst Cassirer, *The Myth of the State* (New Haven, 1946), pp. 45–46.

46. *Ibid., p. 298.*

4. A Left-Wing Identity

1. D. A. Prater, *European of Yesterday: A Biography of Stefan Zweig* (Oxford, 1972), p. 308.

2. Stefan Zweig, *Briefe an Freunde,* ed. Richard Friedenthal (Frankfurt am Main 1978), pp. 132–33.

3. Istvan Deak, *Weimar Germany's Intellectuals* (Berkeley and Los Angeles, 1968), pp. 24–29.

4. *Ibid.,* p. 24.

5. George L. Mosse, "German Socialists and the Jewish Question in the Weimar Republic," *Masses and Man* (New York, 1980), ch. 15.

6. Ernst Bloch, *Auswahl aus seinen Schriften* (Frankfurt am Main, 1967), p. 158.

7. Andrew Arato and Paul Breines, *The Young Lukács and the Origins of Western Marxism* (New York, 1979), pp. 214–15.

8. Martin Jay, *The Dialectical Imagination: A History of the Frankfurt School and the Institute of Social Research, 1923–1950* (Boston, 1973), p. 34;

Russell Jacoby, "Marxism and the Critical School," *Theory and Society* 1(1974):231–38.

9. Arato and Breines, *The Young Lukács*, p. 138.

10. Max Horkheimer and Theodor Adorno, *Dialektik der Aufklärung* (Amsterdam, 1947), p. 53.

11. *Ibid.*, p. 63.

12. Barry Kātz, *Herbert Marcuse and the Art of Liberation* (London, 1982), p. 100.

13. Quoted in George Friedman, *The Political Philosophy of the Frankfurt School* (Ithaca and London, 1981), p. 187.

14. Jay, *The Dialectical Imagination*, p. 33.

15. Deak, *Weimar Germany's Intellectuals*, p. 29.

16. Arato and Breines, *The Young Lukács*, p. 212.

17. *Ibid.*, p. 224.

18. Paul Breines, "Marcuse and the New Left in America," in Jurgen Habermas, ed., *Antworten auf Herbert Marcuse* (Frankfurt am Main, 1968), p. 146.

19. Herbert Marcuse, *One-Dimensional Man: Studies in the Ideology of Advanced Industrial Society* (Boston, 1964), p. 57.

20. Herbert Marcuse, *Kultur und Gesellschaft,* vol. 1 (Frankfurt am Main, 1967), ch. 17.

21. Jürgen Habermas, *Philosophisch-Politische Profile* (Frankfurt am Main, 1971), p. 45.

22. George L. Mosse, *Germans and Jews* (New York, 1970), pp. 179–80.

23. Alfred Enseling, *Die Weltbühne* (Münster, 1962), p. 94.

24. *Ibid.*, pp. 185–86.

25. Leonhard Frank, *Der Mensch ist gut* (Potsdam, 1919), p. 74.

26. Thomas E. Willey, *Back to Kant* (Detroit, 1978), p. 104; Kurt Eisner, *Die Halbe Macht den Räten,* ed. Renate and Gerhard Schmolze (Köln, 1969), *passim.*

27. Mosse, *Germans and Jews,* ch. 7.

28. Walter Benjamin to Ludwig Strauss, 11 September 1912. Jewish National and University Library, Jerusalem, Archives Ms. Var. 424, 196/9, pp. 2–3.

29. Walter Benjamin to Ludwig Strauss, 7 January 1913. Jewish National and University Library, Jerusalem, Archives Ms. Var. 424, 196/9, p. 3.

30. Jay, *The Dialectical Imagination,* p. 198.

31. *Ibid.*, p. 201.

32. Gershom Scholem, *Walter Benjamin—die Geschichte einer Freundschaft* (Frankfurt am Main, 1975), p. 173.

33. Robert Weltsch, "Deutscher Zionismus in der Rückschau," *An der Wende des modernen Judentums* (Tübingen, 1972), p. 53.

34. Mosse, *Masses and Man,* p. 294.

35. Istvan Deak, *Weimar Germany's Left-Wing Intellectuals,* pp. 183–84.

36. George Lichtheim, *Lukács* (London, 1970), especially ch. 5.

37. E.g., T. W. Adorno, "Scientific Experiences of a European Scholar in America," in Donald Fleming and Bernard Baylin, eds., *The Intellectual Migration* (Cambridge, 1969), pp. 340 ff.

38. George L. Mosse, *Towards the Final Solution* (New York, 1978), pp. 178–79.

39. Marjorie Lamberti, *Jewish Activism in Imperial Germany* (New Haven, Conn., 1978), pp. 25 ff.

40. Jakob Wassermann, *Mein Weg als Deutscher und Jude* (Berlin, 1921), pp. 115–16.

41 George L. Mosse, "Jewish Emancipation between *Bildung* and *Sittlichkeit*," in Jehuda Reinharz and Walter Schatzberg, eds., *The Jewish Response to German Culture* (Hanover, New Hampshire, 1985).

42. Ismar Schorsch, "Art as Social History: Oppenheim and the German-Jewish Vision of Emancipation," *Moritz Oppenheim, The First Jewish Painter* (Israel Museum, Jerusalem, 1983), *passim*. The Jews who were disciples of the poet Stefan George also challenged the respectability of German Jewry, abandoning the humanitarian Enlightenment for an emotional, although disciplined, poetic view of the world. This has been brilliantly sketched in only a few pages by Hans Liebeschütz, "Ernst Kantorowicz and the George Circle," *Yearbook IX* (Leo Baeck Institute, 1964), pp. 345–47. This movement did not outlive Nazi Germany.

43. Maurizio Serra has analyzed in a fascinating manner the controversy of the tyranny of history over the minds of men during the 1930s in "Sui miti fascisti e la crisi storica dell'umanesimo borghese negli anni trenta," *Storia Contemporanea* 14 (October 1983):577–603.

V: The End and a New Beginning?

1. Uwe Dietrich Adam, *Judenpolitik im Dritten Reich* (Düsseldorf, 1972), p. 125, n. 63.

2. Michael H. Kater, "Erkenntnisstreben oder Obskurantismus? Kritisches über neuere Literatur zur Sozialgeschichte Deutschlands seit 1879," *Archiv für Sozialgeschichte* 21 (1981):575.

3. Alfred Kerr, "Die Diktatur des Hausknechts," in *Die Welt im Licht*, Friedrich Luft, ed. (Köln and Berlin, 1961), p. 385.

4. Caesar Seligmann, *Festpredigt zur Jahrhundertfeier des Philantrophin*, 16 April 1904 (Hamburg, n.d.), p. 4.

5. *Ibid.*, p. 3.

6. *Ibid.*, p. 5.

7. Michael A. Meyer, "Caesar Seligmann and the Development of Liberal Judaism in Germany at the Beginning of the Twentieth Century," *Hebrew Union College Annual*, vol. 40–41 (1969–70), p. 543.

8. Hans Kohn, "Zionism Is Not Judaism," reprinted in Paul R. Mendes-Flohr, ed., *A Land of Two Peoples: Martin Buber on Jews and Arabs* (Oxford, 1983), p. 97.

9. Martin Buber, "And If Not Now, When?" (July 1932), reprinted in Mendes-Flohr, ed., *A Land of Two Peoples*, p. 104.

10. *Jüdische Rundschau*, no. 59 (25 July 1933), p. 365.

11. Jehuda Reinharz, "Martin Buber's Impact on German Zionism before World War I," *Studies in Zionism*, no. 6 (Autumn 1982): 182.

12. *Ibid.*, p. 183.

13. Hans Kohn, *Living in a World Revolution* (New York, 1964), p. 48.

14. Samson Raphael Hirsch, "Worte bei der Schulfeier der Unterrichtsanstalt der Israelitischen Religionsgemeinschaft zu Frankfurt am Main den 9. November 1859, am Vorabend der Schillerfeier" (Frankfurt am Main, 1905), pp. 5, 11.

15. Julius Bab, "Kulturbund Deutscher Juden," *Der Schild* 12 (14 September 1933): 148.

16. For an account of the *Kulturbund* from a Nazi point of view, see Hans Hinkel, ed., *Judenviertel Europas* (Berlin, 1939), pp. 12–14.

17. Reichskulturwalter Hinkel to the *Nationalsozialistische Partei-Korrespondenz*, quoted in the *Frankfurter Zeitung*, no. 129/40 (13 May 1937). Jüdischer Kulturbund, *Spielplan für Frankfurt am Main* (1936). Wiener Library, Tel Aviv, Jüdischer Kulturbund, Box 4. For the career of Hans Hinkel, who eventually played a role in the deportation of Jews from Berlin and Vienna, see Willi A. Boelcke, ed., *Kriegspropaganda 1939–1941, Geheime Ministerkonferenzen im Reichspropagandaministerium* (Stuttgart, 1966), pp. 85–88. I owe this reference to Alan E. Steinweis.

18. Letter to Propaganda Amt, Kreisleitung I, Gauleitung NSDAP Berlin, to Propagandaleiter Hicketier, 19 November, 1934. Wiener Library, Tel Aviv, Jüdischer Kulturbund, Box 1.

19. E.g., Hinkel, ed., *Judenviertel Europas*, p. 14.

20. For the background of the Nazi theater, see Boguslaw Drewniak, *Das Theater im NS-Staat. Szenarium deutscher Zeitgeschichte 1933–1945* (Düsseldorf, 1984).

21. "Zur Kulturbund-Tagung," *Jüdische Rundschau*, no. 43 (11 April 1936).

22. Walter Perl, "Jettchen Gebert," 11 June 1935. Wiener Library, Tel Aviv, Jüdischer Kulturbund, Box 3. The novel was performed as a play that same year.

23. "Gegenwart und Zukunft der Jüdischen Literatur," *Der Morgen*, 12 (September 1936):260. I owe this reference to Itta Shedletzky.

24. *Israelitisches Familienblatt* (10 September 1936).

25. Marion Kaplan, *The Jewish Feminist Movement in Germany* (Westport, Conn., 1979), p. 205.

26. "Zur Kulturbund-Tagung," *Jüdische Rundschau*, no. 43 (11 April 1936).

27. Ismar Schorsch, "Art as Social History: Oppenheim and the German Jewish Vision of Emancipation," *Moritz Oppenheim, The First Jewish Painter* (Israel Museum, Jerusalem, 1983), p. 51.

28. Herbert Freeden, *Jüdisches Theater in Nazideutschland* (Tübingen, 1964), pp. 94–95.

29. *Der Morgen*, 11 (April 1935):21.

30. *Verkaufskatalog 1940*, Jüdischer Kulturbund, *passim*.

31. I. Herzberg, *Moses Mendelssohn, ein Lebensbild für die israelitische Jugend* (Leipzig, 1929), pp. 84, 90.

INDEX

Adorno, Theodor, 58, 59, 61, 66, 68
Aesthetics, 6–7, 58–59
Anti-Semitism, 11, 22, 43, 61, 67, 72
Apocalyptic tradition, 34–35
Arendt, Hannah, 15
Arndt, Ernst Moritz, 9
Art history, 50–51
Auerbach, Berthold, 4, 5, 10, 24, 25, 26, 29, 32, 39, 46

Bab, Julius, 16, 78
Baeck, Leo, 23, 29
Barfüssle (Auerbach), 5
Beardsley, Aubrey, 23
Bebel, August, 67
Benjamin, Walter, 14, 59, 61, 66–67
Bergmann, Hugo, 77
Bernhard, Georg, 17
Bielschowsky, Albert, 45
Bildung
  aesthetics and, 6–7, 58–59
  the bourgeoisie and, 11–12
  the classics and, 53
  decline of, 5–6, 13–14, 17–18
  definition of, 3, 12
  in drama, 15–17
  friendship cult, 10–11, 15–16
  German classics and, 43–47
  in German-Jewish consciousness, 4
  individuality, 9–10
  institutionalization of, 12–13
  inward process of, 3
  irrationality and, 50–52
  Jewish alienation and, 8
  Jewish commitment to, 14–15, 42–43, 46, 80–81
  Jewish identity, effect on, 7–8, 52
  left-wing intellectuals' interest in, 63
  literature promoting, 19–20
  National Socialism and, 73–74
  politics and, 18
  in popular culture, 29–30, 32–33, 36
  presuppositions of, 6
  religion and, 4, 5, 18–19, 42

socialism and, 56, 59–60
Zionism and, 76–77
Bildungsbürgertum, ix, 9, 14, 22–23, 32, 42, 43, 45, 49, 61
Bing, Gertrud, 51, 52
Bismarck (Ludwig), 27
Bloch, Ernst, 12, 15, 34, 35, 57
Blumenfeld, Kurt, 14, 76
Böhme, Jacob, 34
Bolshevism, 68–69
Bourgeoisie, 11–12
Buber, Martin, 27, 35, 36, 37, 39, 44, 47, 50, 75, 76

Capitalism, 59
Caspar Hauser (Wassermann), 37, 38
Cassirer, Ernst, 53, 54, 71
Central-Verein deutscher Staatsbürger judischen Glaubens (C. V. Zeitung), 2, 16, 17, 19
Churchill, Winston, 68
Cohen, Hermann, 44
Council of the wise, 64–65
Critical theory, 60, 61
Cultural ghetto, 78, 79

Deak, Istvan, 61
Deutsche Bildungswesen, Das (Paulsen), 12
Diktatur des Hausknechts, Die (Kerr), 73

Eisner, Kurt, 64, 65, 66, 68
Ekstein, Modris, 17
Eminent Victorians (Strachey), 28
Erasmus (Zweig), 30, 31

Feuchtwanger, Lion, 66, 68
Fichte, Johann Gottlieb, 12, 13, 43–44, 75
Fontane, Theodor, 11
France, 17–18, 43, 61
Frank, Leonhard, 65
Frankfurt school (Institute for Social Research, University of Frankfurt), 59, 60, 61–62, 63, 66, 68
Freud, Sigmund, 48–49, 50

Friendship cult, 10–11, 15–16
Fürhrer Europas nach der Natur gezeichnet (Ludwig), 30

Ganghofer, Ludwig, 33
Gänsemännchen (Wassermann), 37–38
Gartenlaube, Die (journal), 33–34
Geiger, Ludwig, 10, 45
German classics, 43–47
German wars of liberation, 8–9
German-Jewish dialog, 1–2, 56
Gilbert, Yvetie, 17
Goethe, Johann Wolfgang von, 3, 7, 10, 43, 44–46
Gordon, Aron David, 77
Greek culture, 6, 9–10, 14
Gundolf, Friedrich, 46

Ha-am, Ahad, 76
Hasidic stories, 35–37
Hegel, Georg W. F., 64
Heine, Heinrich, 45, 81
Herder, Johann von, 3, 4, 43, 75
Hermann, Georg, 69, 79
Hinkel, Hans, 78–79
Hirsch, Samson Raphael, 77
Historical biographies
    Bildung, promotion of, 29–30, 32–33
    critical, 27–28
    importance of, 40–41
    of Jews, 29
    leadership, admiration of, 30
    masses, depiction of the, 31–33
    politics, depiction of, 33
    popularity of, 25–27, 28, 31
    psychological, 27
Hitler, Adolf, 34–35, 72, 73
Horkheimer, Max, 58, 59, 61, 68
Humboldt, Wilhelm von, 6, 7, 8, 9, 11, 12, 13, 56

Im Westen nichts neuese (Remarque), 31
Intellectuals, 49–50
    See also Left-wing intellectuals
Irrationality, 47, 50–54

Jay, Martin, 61
Jettchen Gebert (Hermann), 69
Jewish culture under National Socialism, 78–81
Jewish identity
    Bildung, effect of, 7–8, 52
    redefinition of, 2
    religion and, 18–19
Jewish literature, 79, 81
Jewish orthodoxy, 77

Jews
    alienation of, 8
    assimilation of, 45
    emancipation of, 2–3, 10–11
    German-Jewish identity, 80
    isolation of, 72
    middle-class orientation, 69–70
    National Socialism, failure to comprehend, 72–74
    as outsiders, 14, 24
    patriotism of, 8–9
    political activity, 18, 22
    social structure, 4–5
    See also Left-wing intellectuals
Judaism
    German culture and, 74–75, 77–81
    nationalism and, 75–77
Jude, Der (journal), 31
Juden, Die (Lessing), 10
Jüdische Kulturbund. See Kulturbund Deutscher Juden
Jüdische Rundschau (newspaper), 75
Jüdischer Frauenbund, 80

Kafka, Franz, 40
Kant, Immanuel, 34, 64
Kätz, Barry, 60
Kerr, Alfred, 73
Klopstock, Friedrich Gottlieb, 9
Kohn, Hans, 75, 77
Kulturbund Deutscher Juden, 16, 43, 75, 78–80, 81

Lachmann-Mosse, Hans, 17
Landauer, Gustav, 36
Left-wing intellectuals
    Bildung, interest in, 63
    as conscience of the working class, 64–65
    cultivation of the mind, 59–60
    heritage of, 70–71
    isolation of, 67–68
    Jewish opposition to, 68–70
    Jewishness of, 61–62, 65–67
    Kant, interest in, 64
    Marxism and, 57–58
    party affiliations, 56
    revolutionization of society, 60–61
    socialism and, 55–57, 58–59
    "totality of life" concept, 62
    transcendence, search for, 60
    Weimar culture, influence on, 22, 23
Lessing, Gottlob Ephraim, 9, 10, 15–16, 46, 52
Lessing monuments, 15
Leviné, Eugen, 68
Liberalism, 63–64

Löns, Hermann, 5
Ludwig, Emil, 20, 24–25, 26, 27–28, 29–30, 31–32, 33, 39, 40, 41, 50
Lukács, Georg, 35, 57, 58, 59, 62, 68, 71

Mann, Heinrich, 18
Marcuse, Herbert, 62–63
Marcuse, Ludwig, 13
Marlitt (Eugenie John), 33
Marx, Karl, 57, 63, 64
"Marx and Kant" (Eisner), 64
Marxism, 57–58, 60, 62
Massenpsychologie und Ich-Analyse (Freud), 49
Maybaum, Ignaz, 4
Mediation, 59
Mein Weg als Deutcher und Jude (Wassermann), 38, 69
Mendelssohn, Moses, 10, 15, 81
Mensch ist gut, Der (Frank), 65
Menschensohn, Der (Ludwig), 31
Morgen, Der (journal), 80
Myth of the State (Cassirer), 53, 54
Mythology
  fantasy and, 53
  of German political right, 47–48
  of Jewish *Volk*, 47
  political, 54
  rational analysis of, 48–50

Nathan der Weise (Lessing), 9, 15–17, 40, 43, 73, 75, 79
National Socialism, 72–74, 78–81
Nationalism, 13–14, 42, 75–77
New Left, 62–63, 70–71
Nietzsche, Friedrich, 51
Nobel, Nehemia Anton, 46

One-Dimensional Man (Marcuse), 62–63
Oppenheim, Moritz, 8, 10, 69, 80

Panofsky, Erwin, 53
Paracelsus (T. von Hohenheim), 34
Paulsen, Friedrich, 12
Philippson, Ludwig, 8
Philosophy and irrational activity, 53–54
Political right, 47–48
Politics, 18, 22, 33, 54
  See also Left-wing intellectuals
Popular culture
  apocalyptic tradition, 34–35
  Bildung in, 29–30, 32–33, 36
  experimentation in, 22–24
  German-Jewish contact through, 39–40
  German-Jewish heritage in, 25–26
  Hasidic stories, 35–37

historical biographies, 25–33, 40–41
Jewish writers, popularity of, 24–25
liberal nature of, 33–34
mysticism, 35–37
*Volk*ish vision, 37–39
Psychoanalysis, 49

Rathenau, Walther, 26, 29, 35
Reden an die deutsche Nation (Fichte), 44
Religion, 4, 5, 18–19, 42
Remarque, Erich Maria, 31
Riesser, Gabriel, 15, 46
Rolland, Romain, 50

Salomon, Gotthold, 7
Schiller, Friedrich, 7, 44
Schleiermacher, Friedrich, 13
Scholarship
  irrationality, confrontation with, 47, 50–54
  mythology and, 47–49
  ordering function of, 53
  rationality and, 52
Scholem, Gershom, 36, 67
Schorsch, Ismar, 69
Schrift und Volk (Auerbach), 4, 5, 25
Seligmann, Caesar, 15, 74–75, 77
Socialism, 55–57, 58–60, 64–66
Steinthal, Heymann, 80
Sternstunden der Menschheit (Zweig), 28
Strachey, Lytton, 28
Strauss, Ludwig, 14
Sulamith (journal), 3, 6, 7, 18, 48

Thälmann, Ernst, 68
Thomas Müntzer (Bloch), 34, 35
Toller, Ernst, 65, 66
Transcendence, 60
Traumdeutung, Die (Freud), 48
True consciousness, 63

Varnhagen, Rahel von, 45–46
Volk, 37–39, 47, 76

Wagner, Richard, 23
Warburg, Aby, 50–52, 53, 71
Warburg Library, 50, 52, 53
Wassermann, Jakob, 37–39, 69
Wehrwolf, Der (Löns), 5
Weitling, William, 34
Welt von Gestern, Die (Zweig), 40–41
Weltbühne, Die (journal), 56, 64, 68, 71
Weltsch, Robert, 44, 75, 76
Werner, Cossmann, 19
Wesen des Judentum, Das (Baeck), 23
Wieland, Christoph Martin, 10

Wilhelm Meister's Apprenticeship (Goethe), 3, 10
Wolf, Joseph, 11
Wolff, Theodor, 17
Wynecken, Gustav, 23

Zionism, 36–37, 75–77
Zionists, 16, 44
Zweig, Arnold, 49, 50
Zweig, Stefan, 19–20, 24–25, 26–27, 28, 29, 30–31, 32–33, 38–41, 50, 56

GEORGE L. MOSSE is Weinstein-Bascom Professor of Jewish
Studies at the University of Wisconsin-Madison and Koebner
Professor of History at the Hebrew University. He is the
author of many books, including *Germans and Jews* and
Towards the Final Solution: A History of European Racism.